THE USES OF ADVERSITY

Survival of a Woman in the Twentieth Century.

Copyright © **Jeremy Seabrook**, 2014

Jeremy Seabrook has asserted his right under the Copyright, Designs and Patterns Act, 1988 to be identified as the author of this work. This novel is a work of fiction. Names and characters are the product of the author's imagination and any resemblance to actual persons, living or dead, is entirely coincidental.

This book is sold subject to the condition that it shall not, by way of trade or otherwise, be lent, resold, hired out, or otherwise circulated without the publisher's written consent in any form of binding or cover other than that in which it is published and without a similar condition, including this condition, being imposed on the subsequent purchaser.

Typeset for print by Electric Reads

www.electricreads.com

'Sweet are the uses of adversity
Which, like the toad, ugly and venomous,
Wears yet a precious jewel in his head.'

- Shakespeare, As You Like It.

Foreword

Syphilis, to the first half of the twentieth century, was regarded by society much as HIV/AIDS was in the 1980s. The principal difference was that syphilis remained the object of a rigorous taboo. It was a private and lonely torment to the individuals it touched. Those who suffered were at that time in no position to struggle against the public shame to which they would have been exposed, had it become known.

My family's life was shadowed by is secret ravages, which extended far beyond the damaging physical effects. This story is about the response of one woman, my mother, to her husband, when she discovered he had contracted syphilis. I offer this account of her life with affection for all the protagonists, in the hope that the time has now come when no sickness, no disability, no plague, no syphilis and no HIV/AIDS will ever again be thought of as deserved by those affected by it.

Some of the passages in this book have been published by GRANTA, for which I would like to acknowledge my warm thanks to Ian Jack.

Jeremy Seabrook
London
April 2014

Contents

Foreword 5

Prologue 9

Part One 13

Part Two 51

Part Three 91

Part Four 119

Part Five 165

THE USES OF ADVERSITY

PROLOGUE

A funeral is always a good place to begin, even though there was nothing remarkable about the spare ceremony of my mother's cremation. The crematorium was said to have been given as a macabre twenty-first birthday present to his son by its owner, a prudent entrepreneur who had foreseen in the 1920s that burning, not burying, was the coming thing. The building was a bleak red-brick structure, its style only vaguely ecclesiastical, perhaps in order not to remind people too strongly of the doctrine of the resurrection of the flesh.

My mother was eighty six, and the last of twelve siblings. I was content for the officiant (was he a minister?) to note down a public outline of her life, and to tell the tiny congregation about it, which he did verbosely, fruitily, as though he were the bereaved and the rest of us merely bystanders. He knew nothing of her, and during my hour-long interview with him, I took good care that he would remain innocent of any intimate knowledge of her poignant story. I relished the bland insipidity of his address, which made it sound as though nothing significant had happened to her, apart from her extensive birth-family and her twin sons; although if he had looked closely at the depleted attendance, he would have observed that my brother and his wife had seated themselves at the back of the chapel, in order to maintain a proper sense of detachment from an event in which a display of grief on their part would have appeared hypocritical and

9

unconvincing.

They had not seen her since she went to live with them, briefly, some seven years earlier. Within a few months she was making desperate calls to relatives to fetch her home to the terraced house where she had lived with her sister for thirty three years, and which we had presciently not sold, half-aware of the possibility of her return. She had felt isolated in the remote converted parsonage in which my brother lived. It had been a mistake and she begged to be brought back to Northampton, to where, as she said, the remains of her life were. Her own flesh and blood, she observed grimly, had offered less security than her own bricks and mortar.

My cousin and her husband fetched my mother and her sister from their exile on my mother's eightieth birthday. We had arranged temporary accommodation for them in two small rooms in what we had known as children as the 'Fever Hospital'; a rambling Victorian structure then on the outskirts of town, where people with fearful infections were quarantined from the robustly healthy. Whenever we passed by, we held our breath, still in thrall to an ancient superstition that 'fevers' – I suppose cholera and typhoid – were borne on the air. But by the 1980s, it had been transformed, and the two elderly women, exhausted after the emotional upheaval and the long journey, were comfortably installed in a small room with a picture window and a view of the fir trees over which the westering sun lingered in the June evenings.

The house would have to be adapted to receive them; scoured and swept to remove the sour smell of dust from floors which they had once prided themselves you could eat off. A commodity called a 'care package' would have to be arranged with the local authority. They moved back into the house they had believed vacated for ever, a shameful homecoming, since they had departed, ceremoniously, to spend the evening of their days in the tranquil refuge of a home that had recently served spiritual purposes. Neighbours called and asked

The Uses Of Adversity

indirect questions. 'Nice to see you home'; 'I knew you'd never settle.' They remained in Palmerston Road for a further three years, as residents older than themselves died, houses were acquired by the council for 'short-term lets' and the respectable increasingly deserted it for exurban estates. Reluctantly, when they could no longer negotiate what had become hazards in the place they called home – stairs, cooking stove, gas-fire – for a third of a century, they permitted themselves to be moved into a nursing home, even though my mother said that into those two words three lies were compressed. There was scant nursing, it wasn't a home, and could not therefore claim to be a nursing-home.

I had not spoken to my brother for many years. On my rare visits to the old ladies in the country, I had been directed to the side-entrance, so I would not have to walk through the house.

My twin and his wife stood on the edge of the crematorium grounds, as though to emphasize their detachment from the ceremony. The grey October afternoon, clouds lined with smoky orange from the late sun, was pierced by the cawing of rooks, and the withered hands of horse-chestnut leaves fluttered onto the condolence area and the pergola beneath which meagre floral tributes were displayed. I approached my brother and extended a hand. He had said 'I'll shake your hand, and then that's it,' making it clear this would be the limit of any communication between us.

And so it was. As soon as the coffin, squeaking on un-oiled grooves into the furnace behind discreet blue curtains, had been consigned to the scientifically controlled flames that would reduce it to vapour and ash, they disappeared. It was the last time I saw him. It was a day for affirming separations – the parting from our mother was not unexpected; the division between my brother and me had been established from birth, and if we had made efforts to bridge it, these proved less effective than her determination to keep us apart, bewildered strangers who were twins.

Jeremy Seabrook

PART ONE

I

My mother's whole life had tended towards the complete immobility which claimed her in the end. She had always been afraid of going away or leaving home for any purpose. She found good reasons not to take a holiday, to remain behind, above all, *to stay indoors*. 'No, you go', she would say with the generosity of those who renounce things they do not care for. When we were children, she was always at home. If seemed that home was her element, the only place in which she felt safe. She used to say 'I never go anywhere', as though in obedience to some long vanished law of settlement were the highest virtue. Later, seized by agoraphobia, she became terrified even of going outside the house, and then of going upstairs, and finally, of getting up from her chair. And at last, rigid with arthritis, and at the same time, shaking with Parkinson's disease, she was stranded. She could do nothing without help. She was still at last.

But the security of remaining in one place was not what she really sought, for it brought her neither peace nor contentment. The search for stillness had, at its source, an extreme inner turbulence, an unquiet agitation which had never known rest. But her disturbed spirit expressed itself in highly concrete anxieties: If I leave the house, I might have an accident, I might fall in the street; and it was partly the social shame of such an eventuality that confined her. She was convinced that if she went away, something terrible would happen. She had a horror of anything that was unexpected, sudden or improvised. It was, of course, an aspect of her need to keep control, to maintain the illusion that she was the prime mover, not only in her own life, but in the lives of those around her.

Even when she was completely paralysed, the anxiety did not recede. In the nursing home where she spent the last two years of her life, her questions were What if the nurses drop me, what if they don't hear when I cry out in the night? Her desire to be at rest was only a metaphor for the internal turbulence that was unaffected by the apparently total repose of her last years.

The cramped life, constrained by fear, continued to trouble her until she died. An intelligent and able woman, she always maintained it was a lack of education that had handicapped her, but this was only a story to cover a truly disabling affliction.

What was she afraid of in the world beyond the narrow scope of her restricted mobility? Relatives would cajole her into a bus-ride to the sea, a day out in the country, once or twice even into a holiday abroad. Sometimes she would yield, but afterwards said 'I didn't enjoy it. I shan't go again.'

Her reluctance to participate appeared as aloofness, as though she disdained ordinary pleasures. She gave the impression of one so bowed down by her own grief – a sorrow which, however, she never defined – that it made everything else appear trivial.

One day, when I was about fourteen, her sister persuaded her to go to the cinema, the Savoy, where we sat in the carpeted sweep of the balcony, in muted pink lighting which cast a misty sheen over the photographs of Margaret Lockwood and Anna Neagle on the cream-painted walls. The film was *So Little Time*, with Marius Goring and Maria Schell, and told the story of an impossible wartime romance in Belgium between an occupying Nazi officer and the daughter of the chateau which had been requisitioned by the Germans. It was a forbidden and doomed love between the Nazi

The Uses Of Adversity

officer and the young Belgian whose male relatives had been killed by the enemy. I was so unaccustomed to being with my mother in so frivolous a setting that I kept looking at her to see if she was enjoying the experience. I realised she was devastated by the emotions it released in her. Her whole face was wet with tears, as she tried to prevent the sobs from shaking her body. I was frightened by this abandon, a release of feeling I had never witnessed. I understood that she was terrified by something in herself. I could not judge until many years later, the identification she had found between her own life and the fateful relationship on screen.

When the film was over, she was disparaging. 'Lot of rubbish.' But she never went to the pictures again. She stayed at home more and more, in the house that was to her a house of industry, a place of containment for the disordered emotions within.

II

She had been taken out of school on her fourteenth birthday to work in a brush factory. Her job was to operate the treadle that pulled bristles through the wooden base of the broom. She was rescued by the authorities, because it had recently become the law that children were to remain at school until the end of the term in which their fourteenth birthday fell; perhaps it was felt too unceremonious to make them quit on their birthday. Whatever the cause, her schooling was prolonged by this benign legislation for a further six weeks, and this qualified her for clerical work in the office of a boot factory. One day, as she ran down the street, late for work, a neighbour stopped her. 'I shouldn't rush, duck. They won't be wanting you today.' The factory had been burned down; a familiar occurrence during depressed times, according to the shoe-workers, since the owners found it more profitable to draw insurance money than to continue to pay the operatives.

When she spoke of her school in later life, my mother recalled with pride that during sewing classes, it had been the custom to have one pupil read to the others as they worked, and that she was invariably selected for the privilege. As a result, she knew long passages of Wordsworth, Tennyson and Christina Rossetti by heart. The negative consequence of her ability to read with feeling was that her sewing skills were meagre; although this did not prevent her, when my brother and I were small, from sitting long hours by the dying fire late at night, darning our socks held taut over a pink wooden mushroom.

She belonged to a generation who still revered their teachers. I felt I was personally acquainted with the Miss Parnell who had exercised so powerful and tender an influence upon her; my mother said 'She opened my eyes to the world.' When she recited her poems, I could hear the long-dead schoolmistress in the inflections of my mother's voice. Of course, my mother passed the exam to go to the Grammar School. Of course, there was no question of her going, because the family were so poor. 'I thought it was Grandma School, and used to wonder what I would do with a lot of Grandmas. I ran home and told my mother 'I'm going to the Grandma School.' She looked at me, kissed and said 'No, you're not, my duck.'

My mother had little inclination for domestic tasks, and was not very good at them, although her role as woman at that time compelled her to claim competences which, it was felt, censoriously, that no woman worthy of the name could be without. She never liked cooking, although she insisted that everything she served us was of the finest quality, full of a mysterious quality she called 'goodness.' Mealtimes were functional, not to be associated with pleasure, silent and often lugubrious. Food was bland and without seasoning. She would stand, saucepan in hand, her face flushed with the steam, ladling the best pieces of stewing beef onto

The Uses Of Adversity

my brother's or my plate, leaving for herself only fat and gristle.

She distrusted all forms of enjoyment, above all, anything that suggested exuberance or the release of feelings, which remained, like the budgerigars and canaries which some of our aunts favoured for companionship, strictly caged. This sombre inheritance may have been from her decayed religious beliefs. During her lifetime, she surrendered any faith in the next life, but without ever truly believing in this one; a cultural migration as dramatic as any of the more material journeys made by those who change countries or continents.

She had always seemed to me a sombre, saturnine woman, enclosed in unnamed terrors, which she sought to communicate to my brother and me, without defining them, perhaps in order to provide her with fellowship in her bleak view of the world. This was not a false impression of her, but it was not the whole story. Stories, of course, are, by their nature, never whole. It wasn't until she was in her eighties that I heard her laugh full-throatedly at my cousin's jokes, stories I would never have believed she would even understand, let alone receive with such evident amusement. One day, I visited her in the nursing-home. Her eyes were overflowing with tears of laughter. My cousin had just told her a tale about an elderly couple who had just married. 'It came to the wedding night, and he got undressed quickly and jumped into bed. She was taking her time over it, puffing and wheezing as she took her clothes off. 'Come on', he said 'hurry up.' She turned to him with dignity and said 'I'll have you know I've got acute angina.' 'Thank God for that', he said, 'cos your tits are horrible.'

She had scarcely ever spoken to us about sex; and with good reason, as later appeared; just a few sharp words about keeping ourselves clean and treating women properly. She no doubt thought this did not need to be emphasized; her whole life had been an object lesson to us in the abuse of women.

III

One day when I visited her in the nursing-home, I found her in a state of high agitation. 'Look', she said excitedly, 'see who's sitting over there.' In the dim atmosphere, with its wood panels and displays of artificial delphiniums, across the room, between the television and some noisy parakeets, sat an old woman with watery eyes and wispy white hair; indistinguishable from the other wraiths assembled around the walls. My mother, annoyed that I did not recognise her, cried triumphantly 'It's Pearl.'

Pearl had been one of her husband's fancy-women; although the term, always something of an exaggeration, now seemed downright cruel. But it gave my mother a moment of rare exaltation, because Pearl no longer had any memory. 'She doesn't even know me', said my mother. 'She's lost her senses. Not that she was ever burdened with too many in the first place. She's been telling everyone she was engaged to Sid Seabrook. If she was, he never told her he happened to be married to me at the time. Engaged by him, more like.'

Pearl had been married to a policeman. Sid once took away our toys, which he offered to her as a gift for her children. Not only did he rarely give us anything, but he actually robbed us on that occasion in order to impress his current girl-friend. 'Playing to the gallery', was my mother's contemptuous assessment of it; an expression that accurately characterised Sid's inability to sustain relationships and his enthusiasm for new acquaintances. The stolen toys were little wooden wheelbarrows, in which we wheeled the animals of the neighbourhood – a duck, a cat, even a pig. One day, we had gone out with Sid, and after keeping us waiting on the wall outside the pub while he had a couple of drinks, he took us to Pearl's house. There, we had seen our toys in the backyard. When we reached home, we ran to our mother to tell her what had happened. She went to the house and returned in grim triumph with the stolen objects. Once she had retrieved them, we never played with them again. It was only later that I realised that Sid's removal of these wheelbarrows had great symbolic meaning, since it expressed his resentment of the man who had made them for us. The small incident was charged with an intensity of feeling my brother and I could not, at the time understand; adult emotions locked in battle over something as incongruous as the little painted barrows. They stood in the rain, vivid red and blue, until the paint flaked and the wood rotted.

IV

Illness finally became my mother's identity. She was a sick woman. There was a tradition among working class women that they never really recovered from the menopause; for some it might have been mourning for a sexuality that had never really flowered, a delight in life stifled by want of space to express itself. My grandmother's generation had been even more expressive of loss: they 'went into black' in their forties. My grandmother wore an astrakhan hat, a long black coat and laced boots. Women suffered a non-specific but pervasive ill-being, a visceral vague disorder, over which they shook their heads and mouthed incomprehensible syllables over the heads of children.

This malaise did not abate as the twentieth century advanced, since it coincided with departures of the young from the parental home for more distant places than an adjacent street or nearby suburb. They went abroad or were kept so busy by their work that they could make flying visits home only twice a year, at Christmas and in the summer. They installed a telephone to keep in touch and called every Sunday morning, a faintly pious gesture to honouring their father and mother. They sent school photographs of grand-children against a sky-blue background, a tooth missing, a shy smile; and these stood on the little table next to the cerise cyclamen wilting in the heat from the gas-fire. In the emptiness created by these separations, what was more natural than that illness should become more insistent, without remedy? What had been a persistent sense of feeling less than well became more sharply defined. They were not so well, at best 'fair to middling'; afflicted by dizzy spells, turns, flushes; they came over queer in the bus queue, or had to sit down on a chair brought out to the pavement by shopkeepers. They waited for the prescription renewal to arrive from the doctor's surgery with the hope and expectation with which they had once eagerly anticipated love-letters fluttering onto the front doormat.

My mother developed a mystic communion with her illness. It became a bond, tighter, more exclusive than any other; a lonely, unreachable thing. It was the defining edge of her later years, just s we, her sons, had been in middle life. Although my brother and I had felt her attentions to be onerous and unwanted, it was disconcerting to see ourselves supplanted in her affections by a sickness. The tenderness with which she dwelt on every detail of what was crippling her was eerily evocative of the obsessive concern she had once shown us. She sat silently in the winged armchair in the back room, distant and inattentive to what was going on around her. She was monitoring the progress of the illness within, observing the silent disabling of a self that had been powerful, assertive, heroic. She certainly didn't want to die: she had her complaint to take care of, to cherish and keep from harm.

She was an early victim of the pharmaceuticals industry, repository of psychotropic substances which general practitioners were induced to hand out to people in a society which was itself no longer amenable to change; part of the process of forced adaptation of a generation rendered inflexible by age to altered times, the

The Uses Of Adversity

compulsions of the modern world. She was to experience by turn the euphoria produced by purple hearts, the unnatural placidity created by valium, the sleepy aftermath of mogadon and a host of other somnifers. None of them touched the pain at her heart, and indeed could not be expected to.

V

She had done her best to keep me and my brother close to her, to prevent us from growing up, even to preserve us from being male, since she identified men – not incorrectly – as the source of much of her own unhappiness. She wanted us to herself, and barred the path to any attachment to others, even our grandmother and aunts. Our feelings were never allowed to stray, penned in the thorny enclosure of our relationship with her. She always referred to people outside the already diminished family group as 'other people'. To seek their friendship was betrayal, to look for sustenance among them treachery. They would always let you down, and wanted you only for what they could get out of you. 'Fair-weather friends', she said dismissively, she who had had good cause to test loyalties in the harsh inclemencies of her eighty seven years.

When I finished university, I went home, having failed to choose a career or avail myself of the glittering opportunities supposedly open to me after a three-year sentence in a Cambridge college. I worked in the local library, checking and shelving books and keeping an eye out for dirty old men who sidled up with sibilant requests for books in the 'restricted' stock, like Grace Metalious' Peyton Place and other works likely to deprave and corrupt. In the library, not only did I find warmth and companionability among young women denied the advantages I was supposed to have gained, but I became friendly with a young man who represented the first contact our town had had with a new generation of dissenters, which it called 'beatniks.' It always seemed to me a pity that a town which prided itself on a radical tradition – Charles Bradlaugh emblematic of its scepticism and revulsion against petty orthodoxy – could not even recognise its own heirs and successors; indeed, repudiated them with the indignant virtue of the reformed.

Jack Williams grew his hair long, wore old jeans and was a member of CND. He was sensitive and beautiful, and I harboured for him feelings which, even at the age of twenty one, I could still not acknowledge. One Saturday afternoon, he suggested we should go to London for the weekend. Why not, I said with an assumed nonchalance, because I knew my mother would not countenance such picaresque excursions. I had, I told myself, spent summers in France and Italy; how could there be any objection? Of course I would go with him. He had friends with whom we could crash for the night. 'I'll come round for you this afternoon' he said. 'We'll hitch a lift. It sounded dangerous, exciting, independent.

My mother opened the door to him. She said coldly 'What did you want?' in a tense that rendered any demand impossible. He said 'Jerry and I are going to London.' Grimly, emphasizing the unreal condition in her original question, she told him he'd better come inside. She didn't ask him to sit down. To me she said 'What's this?' 'We're going to London.' 'Who is he?' she asked me, 'and why is he dressed up like something the cat brought in?' She turned to him 'What are you, some kind of tramp?' Then to me 'He's dressed in rags, the way we had to dress when we were little. We ran around with our arses hanging out because we were poor. What's his reason?' There followed a recitation of her selflessness. She had given us the best of everything, Chilprufe vests and Crombie coats, she had humiliated and exhausted herself so we should never have to go through what she did. 'Our mother had to put us to bed at three o'clock in the afternoon, and she hung sacks at the windows and told us it was night, so we shouldn't feel hunger. And you' – on me

The Uses Of Adversity

she turned her grey eyes, beneath the ash of which smouldered a fury she could barely contain – 'all you can think of is going back to what I've struggled to keep you from.' To Jack Williams she said 'He's not going to no bloody London. I don't know who you are, or who your mother is. But if I couldn't send him out looking any better than you do, I'd bloodywell keep him at home. He's not going anywhere.' Jack Williams blushed a deep rose colour, lowered his grieved eyes, said 'All right' and slipped out of the front door. I did nothing to stop him, although I knew how ridiculous it looked. But her passion was not to be doubted; her whole body was shaking with rage. What really disturbed me was not that she thought I hankered after the poverty from which she had delivered me, but that she might have sensed the tentative wandering of my affections, however timidly, towards another. What she did not know, indeed, none of us did at the time, was that Jack Williams' own family circumstances had been as irregular and unorthodox as our own. We might have recognised kinship in our outcast status; but there is rarely a great deal of fellow-feeling among the most wretched.

Later, she said to me by way of extenuation for her anger I only want you to be happy.' The key words were 'I want.' This always irritated me, for reasons which I could not then articulate, but which I now recognise as her fundamental misapprehension of me which this benign desire represented. She didn't recognise that my most obvious characteristic was my capacity for being unhappy. She ought to have done, for it was hers also.

VI

She attributed much of the unhappiness of her life to having grown up poor. This was, for her, a primal myth, and she used it to instil gratitude in me and my brother for having delivered us from a similar fate. She would say 'I've lived poverty. You never have. I've kept it from you.' What she didn't say, but was implicit in everything she did was that I should repay her, not only by being thankful, but also by having nothing to do with poor people. It seems nothing is forgotten so swiftly as a poverty that has been left behind, and to her, it was perverseness that drew me back to it. She had dwelt so graphically and insistently on the cruelties of her own childhood that she had successfully implanted them in me; and then she blamed me for my inability to forget. She felt her arduous climb out of misery removed my right to be concerned about social justice. It was no doubt more complex than that. For while my sympathy with poor people infuriated her, she hated snobbery even more. 'Don't you ever forget where you came from' was followed by 'You'll never know what poverty is because of all I've done for you.' She wanted me to strive for a higher social status, but this was to be inflected by her experience; and when I sought to oblige her, she accused me of betrayal.

She was the youngest of twelve children, of whom ten survived into adult life. She had to struggle for space in the crowded house (or houses, since they were always fleeing bailiffs, creditors and moneylenders). To distinguish herself in such a crowd must have required a great effort. She was by no means the most attractive of the seven sisters, but she had two significant advantages, being both the youngest and the cleverest. She always claimed her mother called her 'the flower of my flock'. This was vehemently denied by her sister, with whom we went to live when I was ten. Aunt Em said 'Our mother never made fish of one and fowl of another. She treated us all the same. Glad must have imagined it.' This was as close as Aunt Em ever came to criticising her sister, the sister who found fault with her all the time.

My grandmother was forty five when Glad was born. This meant that her upbringing was shaped by country people whose own childhood dated from the 1860s and 70s. This made her a socially archaic person from the beginning. She was a repository of belief in ancient lore and superstition, the last vestiges of animism that lingers in country people all over the world, and which had not been completely ousted even by the establishment of centuries of Christianity. Her life was coloured by the pre-industrial psyche of shoe-makers, whose work had been that of domestic artisans, since they fetched the raw material from the manufacturers for whom they worked, and laboured at home with considerable control over their time. They were absorbed by factories later in the 19th century, and a particular shoe-making culture emerged in our town; a stingy, frugal and puritanical age, mercifully short-lived, because by the 1960s, leather and shoemaking had been transferred to southern Europe and from there to more distant places. She lived through these social shifts, and the changes they brought in the character of the people, and found herself in old age, in a world twilit by an entertainment industry which offered distraction from the unacknowledged violence of which they had been victims.

VII

When my mother was about ten, the family lived in Alliston Gardens, at that time one of the most shameful and notorious streets in the town, one of the few from which the respectable working class was almost entirely absent. The three-storey houses with dark underground basements must have been built in the 1830s or 40s; and were still standing in the 1960s, by which time the poverty it represented had become an anachronism. When my mother's family lived there, it housed the most recent migrants to the town, the most feckless. Rooms were let separately with shared privies and a pump in the back yard; by the time I discovered it, the buildings were overgrown with briars, buddleia, and the hearts and bells of convolvulus. Our mother explained their sojourn in this tenement by saying that their father 'had drunk the house away, and all the furniture'; an image which fascinated us, since we found it hard to imagine the liquefaction of such material items. 'I used to walk the long way round to school, so nobody should see where I came from.'

In the room above them lived a middle-aged man and his mother. This woman was so fat she had not been out for many years. Occasionally my grandmother would take her some small treat – a cube of jelly dropped into a cup of hot water, or a not too specked orange she had found on the market. The old woman became ill and close to death. One day my mother was alone in the house. She had been away from school with a cough. Her sister May was at school, and the others were working overtime in the boot factories. Her mother had gone in search of the penny bloater that more often than not constituted their main meal or some wood or other combustible waste for the fire.

Glad was uneasy in the house of transients. She was about ten. Through the thin plaster she could hear the breath of the dying woman, hoarse and laboured. She listened to the voice of her son, a pathetic man who had worked on a brewery dray, but was now incapable of lifting heavy loads. He was tearful and entreating, as he begged his mother not to leave him. Glad was transfixed. Suddenly, the room shook, and there was a fall of plaster, and a large piece of masonry just missed her. When the cloud of dust had settled, she could see the metal leg of a bed protruding through the masonry. It had bored a hole in the floor and dislodged part of the ceiling, so

The Uses Of Adversity

that Glad could see clearly into the room above. The woman's son was now weeping openly and calling for help. She could not stand and witness their distress. She ran up the uncarpeted staircase and into the room, where the woman was lying, tilted to one side in a broken bed that threatened at any moment to subside into the room below. It was impossible to lift the burden. There was no one else in the house. My mother ran down into the road, and begged help of a carter passing by the top of the Gardens. He managed to move the bed, so that it was clear of the rotting floorboards, and would be safe for the duration of the life that was ebbing away. 'I could hear the death-rattle as soon as I turned into the Gardens', her mother said when she came back with her firewood; adding grimly when she saw the damage to their room, 'We might as well have burned the floorboards.'

That was not quite the end of the story. The old woman did die during the following day. The coffin, however, could not be moved down the narrow staircase; and the window had to be removed, and it was lowered on ropes to the cart below, which was to accompany it to a pauper's grave.

They did not wait for the hole in the ceiling to be repaired, since the whole building seemed on the verge of collapse. It is difficult to understand how it managed to endure for a further sixty years. They moved back to the part of town they knew best, and which they had fled only because they could not pay the rent. These removals were so frequent that the memory of landlords could scarcely keep track of their debts, and bailiffs had more serious arrears to address; in any case, distraining my grandmother's goods would have been poor work, since these would not even have yielded s single week's rent.

Jeremy Seabrook

VIII

It was a paradox that in our lives, saturated with sex and its prohibitions, we heard few references to it. But it hovered over us and we felt the constant and ominous beating of its wings. One day my brother and I, in company with an older boy, had seen a man – the father of a boy we knew well – masturbating in his front garden. It was a late summer twilight, and he stood on the crazy paving between the hydrangeas, gently manipulating his erection. He beckoned to our friend, who promptly ran home and told his parents what had happened. My brother and I were more discreet, for we sensed these were confidences our mother might not welcome.

The other boy's parents, however, seemed to think action was called for. They came to our house, somewhat dressed up for the occasion, and discussed it with our mother. There was a long, fierce conversation between the adults, while we were banished from the room. What about the police? I'm not having any child of mine dragged through the courts.' What he needs is a bloody good pasting. 'I can't hit him', protested the father of our friend, a sweet-tempered and generous man. Our mother said decisively 'Well, somebody's got to do something. It'll happen again else.' The designated somebody demurred. 'As a man', she said, 'it's your responsibility.' His wife became indignant. 'Don't you tell him what his responsibility is.' 'Well is it, or isn't it?' 'Jim, it's your duty to go and have it out with him.'

Jim went, leaving behind a tense silence between the two women and the injured parties, to whom the flesh-wound, as it were, was intriguing rather than upsetting. The walk was about ten minutes, across the piece of wasteland overgrown with knapweed and yarrow. Our mother made tea with great ceremony, as though keen to demonstrate that her sense of outrage exceeded theirs. She rattled the spoons in the saucers to nurture her sense of indigna-

The Uses Of Adversity

tion, so it should not perish from want of energy.

When Jim returned, he was smiling cheerfully, which angered my mother. He asked for a cup of tea, repudiating with a gesture their eager questions. After drinking noisily, he set down his teacup and said 'It's all right.' 'How can it be all right after what he's done?' Jim said sagely 'It was the War.' There was a silence. 'What was the War?' my mother asked irritably. 'It was the War. Done this to him. It's left him with a kink. The things he saw. Out there. He can't help it.' 'Did you give him a good hiding?' 'Do I look like someone who's just thrashed somebody? He told me he's under the doctor with his nerves.' 'You mean', our mother said slowly, 'that he's going to get away with it? Never.' 'He's assured me, it will never happen again. It was a momentary blackout. He has no recollection of it whatever, although he knows he's liable to do strange things when he gets these attacks.'

Both women were angry now. They spoke as though Jim were an accomplice. My mother suggested that anybody who would connive at such behaviour wouldn't be beyond doing such things himself. That was too much for Jim's wife, who said 'sufficient to the day is the evil thereof', which lent a scriptural finality to the event. To us our mother said 'Go to bed and forget all about it.' Like many of the things she ordered us to forget, they remained indelible. In any case, I felt obscurely aggrieved that our friend had been the object of the man's attention. Since I was so starved of male influence, I spent much of my youth longing to be touched, or held by a man; a condition exacerbated by the proscription on Sid. At that time, we also knew nothing of the cause for Glad's vehemence towards any sexual aberration. Like so many of the high principles she invoked, these stemmed largely from her own sense of having done wrong.

The incident didn't quite end there. Next day, our friend was asked why his father had spent half an hour walking round the waste ground that separated our house from that of the delinquent.

Clearly, Jim was endowed with a considerable sense of the dramatic: he hadn't confronted him at all.

IX

Perhaps it was because sexual licence appeared as an unwarranted luxury in a society still tormented by insecurity, poverty and hunger that it made so many women of my mother's generation talk slightingly about sex.

They would mutter that they'd be thankful when they'd done their bottom button up for good. They resented the Saturday night martyrdom, and supposed you didn't look on the mantelpiece when you poked the fire. How redolent the ceremonial front bedrooms were, with their cavernous wardrobe and the raised platform of the bed, more catafalque than resting-place, sacrificial altars for the ritual slaughter of women's sexuality. What joyless chambers these were, and how sad the disclaimer of many women, who suggested they had never known either self-expression or delight in their own body. They affected a knowingness and cynical self-abnegation, when they said that sex was solely a male preoccupation. Of women who made a virtue of their abstinence they would say it was easy enough to hold the latch down when nobody was trying to get in. Many women extricated themselves from sex soon after the children were born: this was the function of the widespread mythology with which they surrounded giving birth. When they told their young 'I nearly died having you', this was also a message to their men that they no longer want to submit to his clumsy invasive violence, the breath of which smelled of beer and tobacco. On the other hand, our mother also used to say to my brother and me 'You are the best thing that ever happened to me.' This, which reduced our existence to an event in her life, also carried a deeper

The Uses Of Adversity

charge, unspoken until many years later, that our role was also to redeem her tribulations.

She never really entered into collusive intimacy with other women on the estate where we lived. This set her apart from them, and to her they attributed a wisdom which she had certainly attained, since she knew the value of silence and discretion. Accordingly, women who came into the shop would, in a few words, reveal to her the depths of their loneliness, disappointment or pain, displaying their wounds from the tragic gender war which compelled them to submission and silence. My mother's role – her hands stained with the blood of animals as she dispensed the meagre meat ration of the 1940s, and leaned over the marble counter and her eyes met those of her customers through the needle on the glass fan of the scales – the air of counsellor, judge and receptacle for their sorrows.

One woman, a thin, dark-haired and nervous creature, whose hands were never still, told my mother that their marriage had never been properly consummated. They had been together fifteen years. What could she do? Glad asked if her husband had never made any attempt...? The woman said he had never touched her. She thought perhaps he didn't like it. Naturally, she thought it was her fault. 'I blame myself', she said, with that familiar self-attributed abjection that went unchallenged by men. She said she was afraid she inspired only revulsion in him. And indeed, her whole being expressed this conviction: she hunched her shoulders as she clutched her purse over her stomach, her dark hair lank at the sides of her face.

She came into the shop one day and told my mother that she had met another man. It was at the bus stop. He had been visiting his sister who lived on the estate. They had fallen into conversation, and then swiftly into something deeper. He had told her, in the no doubt long intervals that occurred between buses, that he was married, but unhappy. They had gone out 'for a drink,' a euphemism that had absolutely nothing to do with the slaking of thirst. Somehow, they had quickly confided their unhappiness to each other. Since then, they had met in town two or three times. Only they had nowhere to go. What could she do? There was nowhere on the estate. There was no time. Women always had to account for themselves, be ready with the evening meal, keep the house clean, make sure their children were presentable. The neighbourhood was vigilant, always on the alert for infringements of a moral code which it longed to flout but did not dare. There were no nooks and crannies in people's lives, no vacant spaces. You couldn't use relatives an alibi – they would be the first to denounce you. Where could she go with her man-friend? She had heard of people who went to hotels, but it would cost a fortune and she didn't know how to conduct herself in such public arenas. Mother bent forward over the counter and whispered something in her ear. Another customer came in. The woman lingered while the newcomer was served. When she had gone, my mother passed something over the counter, dull metallic; evidence that my mother's attitude towards sexual wrongdoing was more nuanced and ambivalent than she ever admitted. It was the key to the henhouse which stood on the waste ground close to where we lived; an unerotic tryst perhaps, but guaranteed to be free after dark from the attentions of anyone but fowl-thieves.

X

'Whatever happens, don't let me go into a home', she had implored us as children, embracing us fiercely, 'don't put me in a home.' Weeping, terrified, at the age of six or seven, we had sworn solemnly that we would, could never do anything so heartless. It was not difficult to make such promises at that time. The prospect was more remote than that she would be the one to abandon us, since

The Uses Of Adversity

she had more than once threatened to send us 'to live with Mrs Jones', a notably slovenly mother on the estate; and we had no way of knowing what kind of a welcome we might have received in the household of that symbol of maternal neglect. Preserving her from a home was the equivalent of her own mother, who extracted from her children the faithful promise that they would not let her go to a pauper's grave.

But it was into a home that she went in the end. At the time when she had extracted from us a declaration that we would never consign her to such a place, a home was still seen as the most shameful destination imaginable for the unwanted and rejected of society; a public admission that people could not look after their own, or worse, that their own did not deserve to be cared for by their nominally nearest and dearest. It was still the ultimate function of immediate family 'to close your eyes for you', a gesture which clearly entailed a great deal more than this final service. The web of kinship caught people when they fell; but it also held them captive, and not a few perished in its sticky lattice. Until I was well into my twenties, my mother would sometimes take my hands in hers and, looking at me with her troubled grey eyes, beg me not to let her 'finish up in a home.' She always appeared so hale and alert that even then I could still offer my assurances with a light heart.

And when the time did come, the context in which such sometime scandalous events occurred, had changed, and it seemed the most natural thing in the world. Indeed, she welcomed it. The house which she and my aunt had occupied for thirty five years became hostile, the handles of saucepans caught the cuff of cardigans, the gas-taps failed to turn themselves off, and the frayed carpet left loops of fibre which would catch their slow felted feet; and even the appliances that had been installed to help them answer their modest needs more easily had become unmanageable. They would wait for the nurse to come and put them to bed downstairs, in what had been the front parlour. And her arrival depended upon what misfortunes she had encountered on her round. Sometimes a woman had fallen and broken her thigh, and she couldn't get to my mother ad aunt before eleven o'clock, when their eyes were bruised with fatigue and anxiety. Or she might come at seven thirty, while the sun was still glinting on the windows of the houses behind, when this happened to be the first call on her evening journey. The old women sat, captives in their chairs, waiting, watching the pale loops of cobwebs tremble in the heat from the gas fire, observing the dust settle on tables in which they had once prided themselves you could see your reflection, seeing the brass ornaments clouded by the sour breath of old age. The nurse would tuck them up in bed with a hot water bottle, turn off the light, and some, overcome with pity, would kiss them goodnight.

Although she was resigned to the move to the nursing home, my mother was not happy there. But since she had never been happy anywhere, it would have been foolish to expect anything else. The first home had formerly been the residence of a bootmaker, who had made a fortune out of military boots in the First World War. Our town had always thrived in times of war, not directly and lustily, like the cities which flourished on the manufacture of armaments, but surreptitiously, as though half-ashamed. The home was a redbrick gabled structure, surrounded by sombre evergreens, sculpted laurels and stiff holly, the kind of shelter that had offered privacy to the rich on the healthy Western outskirts of the town, where the prevailing wind would not carry the feral smell of tanneries and glue-factories.

It was hard for her to accept that this would be her penultimate resting-place. Although until this time she had read eagerly and extensively, she no longer felt sufficiently at peace to open a book. But she took with her *Bleak House* and *Mill on the Floss*, two of her favourite novels; the staff would pick them up and say 'Fancy being able to read that'. The books were a kind of protection, to signal to carers that she was in full possession of her faculties and that they should not infantilise or mistreat her. She had been much influenced later in life by books I had brought home from school and university. She discovered with delight Flaubert, Balzac, Stendhal, Zola, Manzoni. She loved Giovanni Verga's stories of the poor of Sicily. She read *Mastro Don Gesualdo,* and especially *The House by the Medlar Tree,* and recognised in them an experience that mirrored that of her own family. She marvelled that anyone could ever have written such things, let alone someone from a country at the other end of Europe.

She came to hate television, its baleful and noisy insistence that smothered like a pillow the griefs and losses of the old people in the home. In any case, she said, it crams too many intense and concentrated emotions in a short time, which make people's own lives empty and insipid by contrast. She knew all about intensity, and was aware that such experiences do not come in neatly tied packages, but inform our lives over long, wearying years. She didn't want her own life, however harsh it may have been, eroded by the entertainment industry.

Whenever I visited, I stored up stories to tell her, but they froze on my lips. Everything from outside was to frivolous, an intrusion upon her inconsolable misery. I would sit, holding the arthritic hand, the forefinger of which was bent back upon itself, wondering how to hasten the passage of the three hours we were to spend together. Everything I wanted to say was crushed by the weight of the power that no longer moved, but seemed all the heavier for its unquiet stillness. She said 'If it wasn't for you, I shouldn't ever want to wake up again.' She still had the ability to reduce me to a desperate, sullen silence; perhaps that was what made of me so desirable a companion.

She had really wanted to attach my brother to her, perhaps because his was too frivolous, one she could not fully understand and certainly could not control. She recognised herself in me, and it was no triumph for her to dominate me. My brother, fugitive that he was, deserted her, and left her no choice but the consolation of her empire over me.

XI

On another occasion, a relative affirmed what my cousin had said, that they 'could have a laugh with Glad.' Incredulous, I asked, 'What do you laugh about.' 'She has us in stitches, with all the gossip, staff, patients, visitors.' In the home was a woman who had formerly been a guide at Althorp House, childhood home of Diana, Princess of Wales. She would intercept people on the threshold of the nursing-home, and order them to wait until the whole party was assembled before she could show them round. Some, impressed by her authority, waited for the absent others to appear. She would conduct people from room to room, an accomplished mistress of ceremonies. 'Of course', she would tell them 'His Lordship will never permit anyone to build in the park. He has as high a notion of his duty to posterity as he does to his forebears.'

One day I recognised someone else I knew in the home. This was the Headmaster of the first school where I taught when I returned to Northampton after university. The school was in one of the poorest estates in town; a place where teachers instructed pupils to learn to hold a brush properly because the only thing they would ever be fit for was sweeping the roads. I had chosen this unpromising site for my career precisely because of its reputation, to further remonstrations of my mother over my perverse attachment to poverty. When the teachers heard that a graduate from Cambridge was to join them, they assumed either that I had had a nervous breakdown or that I must be some kind of child-molester. I arrived for work on my first morning dressed in black jeans and a suede jacket. The Headmaster gravely told me that such attire was inadmissible,

The Uses Of Adversity

since he feared it might be prejudicial to the discipline of the school. I had to go home and change before I could be presented before the children to whom pedagogy in such outlandish gear might have wanted the solemnity it demanded.

The Headmaster didn't recognise me; but since he no longer knew anyone, I shook his hand and exchanged some small conversation with him. He was a decent man, but it seemed at the time when he was appointed Head of the school, an absence of imagination was the primary qualification for the post. In any case, I didn't last long at the school. The distrust of the staff was vindicated, since my capacity to maintain discipline was limited; and I was humiliated by the irruption of other teachers into my classroom who wanted to know what the hell was going on, and I replied weakly that this was a lesson in improvised drama. I should no doubt have profited from my mother's advice in this connection.

The news my mother chose to tell me from the home involved none of the scurrilous tales with which she entertained my cousins. 'We lost three this week. God knows what they're doing to us. Mind you, I can understand anyone giving up the ghost in a place like this.' Sometimes she would look at me anxiously as I was leaving, and say 'I'm sorry I haven't been very good company today. I had a bad night.' One Saturday when I had spent the whole day with her, she said proudly to one of the staff 'I've had a companion today.' To have been described in such impersonal terms made me feel like the vicar.

A shrewd survivor, she made friends with many of the staff. They liked her and talked to her, much as her customers had done formerly. She knew of all the efforts by management to save money, she was aware of occupancy rates, the absence of qualified staff, the minimum legal requirement of staffing levels at night. They called her room the Board Room, because grievances could be safely aired there, even if nothing could be done about them, because there was, of course, no union.

Occasionally when I visited, I felt like an intruder into the conspiratorial relationships she had formed with people she saw daily, and whose presence had become more real for her than attachments in the family. She showed the old sympathies which invited confessions. One woman who had been on holiday with her husband to celebrate forty years of marriage was told on their return home that he was leaving her. Others spoke of their debts, their miscarriages, their children's success, their divorces, their lovers. Perhaps they sensed that my mother' supreme gift lay in her ability to keep secrets; a quality become rare in a time of incontinent taletelling.

XII

'Why ever did you marry Sid?' I asked her. If she had set out to find one so completely alien to her sensibility and interests, she could scarcely have made a more perfect choice. She said 'I always assumed everybody was the same. You just got married, had children and that was it.' She suggested that the society she grew up in produced, not highly differentiated individuals, but people who were judged on their behaviour. She really didn't know that people had different needs and desires. To her, a good wife and mother were public roles. They implied conduct, not forms of satisfaction which would have been wild dreams in the poor, enclosed world in which she had grown. 'I thought life unfolded, it brought its pleasures and sadnesses. I supposed it was predictable. I knew there were good husbands and bad. My Dad was a swine to our mother, he drank and knocked her about. He kept her short of money and long on kids. I thought a good husband was one who didn't smoke or drink, who worked and gave his wife enough money to live on and provide for the children. I thought it was a gamble: you made your bed and you were expected to lie on it.'

In her childhood home, there had been little room for sharp psychological variations. She knew the distinctive characters of her siblings – some were kind, others quarrelsome, they were generous or mean, reserved or sociable. But these were all contained within fixed roles, husband and wife, mother and father, sister and brother, son and daughter. These were the principal determinants upon people, and constrained them within certain limits.

When liberation from these rigid categories came, the price paid was high: as well as discovering the presence of individual needs and wants, they also discerned the disagreeable qualities of those to whom they had been bound by blood and duty. Liberation is always conscious of what it is being freed from; what it is delivering people into is not always plain until long afterwards.

In her lifetime, she was to see the replacement of roles by relationships. Part of my mother's suffering – it was not hers alone, but was shared by millions of voiceless people – came from the collapse of a semi-collective value-system, which had evolved in the industrial period as a protection against some of the harshness of industrial life; it was defeated by one of the most subtle forms of colonialism – the dominant ideology of the society against which it had originally created its own barriers and defences.

XIII

Sid had grown up in a little country town in Buckinghamshire, where his parents had a slaughterhouse and butcher's shop; ramshackle buildings at the top of Midland Road, a heavy Victorian addition to the elegant grey 17th and 18h century structures on the High Street. At the bottom of Midland Road was the railway station and opposite the butcher's shop was a Sparking Plug factory, the only trace of industry in the town where William Cowper composed his hymns and where John Newton wrote *Amazing Grace*, and where, in my childhood, old ladies with wicker baskets walked sedately past bow-windowed shops, with their ladies' companions a few steps behind, bowing graciously to tradespeople, and maintaining social distances that would have required astronomical instruments to measure.

The garden of the house was tessellated with blue and brown tiles, and the red and purple blossoms on rambling fuschia bushes danced in the wind. The house was dark and cavernous. In the kitchen stood a long deal table, where the slaughtermen, taciturn, itinerant and mysterious, drank tea from great tin mugs, while the yellow haunches of bacon hanging from a beam on the ceiling filled the room with a smoky pungency. These men all slept in the front bedroom upstairs, a forbidding chamber that smelled of a mixture of untended masculinity and animal blood.

The town was at that time a somnolent country place surrounded by meadows of wild flowers. Its people spoke with a distinctive raw accent, and lived in rows of tumbledown cottages, where women still made lace on the threshold of their houses and children bathed naked among the bulrushes in the river.

Sid was very attractive as a young man, and was said to have borne a strong resemblance to Henry Fonda, whose flickering image sometimes passed across the grainy screen of the little lopsided Electra Cinema in the High Street. He had left school at fourteen with a sense of social inferiority, for among his duties was the delivery of meat, poultry and game to many of the big houses in the town; places where he was patronised by the wives of doctors, lawyers and country gentry. Later, he would be employed by the gentry as beater in the shooting season, when it would be his job to chase the birds from the bushes so that the shooting party might take aim as they flew into the air above Yardley Chase. Sid took pride in his physical appearance, but was keenly aware of his social and intellec-

The Uses Of Adversity

tual limitations.

He had met my mother in Olney High Street, when she was visiting an older sister, who lived in a tiny cottage with a communal yard behind the main road. She was wheeling her sister's baby in a pram, when Sid accosted her and asked if the baby were hers. Glad was more alert than her sisters, perhaps because she was less attractive than they were, but she had a spirit and vivacity at that time which were attractive. Sid perceived in her an intelligence he lacked; and she saw a beautiful man whose mind she might cultivate. She said she was later reminded of George Bernard Shaw, who responded to Mrs Patrick Campbell's suggestion that they should marry, because with her beauty and his brains they would produce a remarkable child, by saying that the child might have the misfortune to be born with her brains and his beauty.

Since her schooldays, Glad had a reputation for thinking deeply; partly a consequence of her capacity for reflection, but it was reinforced by her sense of melancholy. Most working people accounted for their unwillingness to think too much by declaring that if they did so, they would almost certainly finish up putting their head in the gas-oven. It was important to her to distinguish herself from her brothers and sisters: she required a special destiny. She had no idea just how special it was to become, as she entered the hazy landscape of a relationship, believing all the time that she was merely passing into the familiar terrain of traditional role. When the relationship broke down and brought her unhappiness, she fell back upon the less controvertible role of mother; this gave her security and consolation, and later, a safe place from which to carry out revenge for the injuries she had suffered during the eighteen years her marriage lasted.

XIV

Something of the levity I was to detect in her enjoyment of scabrous jokes in old age must have characterised the years about which I knew nothing, apart from the shoe-box in which the family photographs were stored. There were pictures of my mother and Sid, her sister and fiancé on a motorbike with side-car, the two men bestriding the machine and the women, in cloche hats and rows of beads, crammed into the metal skiff attached to the machine and covered by a length of waterproof fabric. They waved and smiled at cameras, as they set out for Brighton or Blackpool, for high jinks in palais-de-danse and road-houses, lidos and shooting-galleries and other rudimentary sites of pioneering popular amusement in the 1930s. There were anecdotes, too, of prudish landladies who ordered them out of respectable establishments, of crashing the bike into the window of a pawnshop and running off with some trinkets – a crime much mitigated by the unwholesome trade of the pawnbroker.

They took a mortgage on butcher's shop on a new estate on the edge of Northampton. It was one of a crescent of eight shops, pebble-dashed, white-washed, with a flat roof, modern, even futuristic. It was one of a number of developments in Britain which gestured towards a California of fantasy, prompted perhaps by a sequence of golden summers; so naturally, the roof leaked and the concrete swiftly became dingy and leprous. The shop had black and white tiles, a huge black refrigerator that hummed and purred night and day, gleaming steel rails from which haunches of dismembered animals bled gently through rosettes of greaseproof paper onto the display counter below. They had handbills printed, S. Seabrook, Family Butcher, with an emblem of a smudgy blue sheep at the top on the paper. I always read the words 'family butcher' with some misgiving, for their ambiguity hinted at a particularly disagreeable

The Uses Of Adversity

form of mass slaughter; and, although I couldn't know it, announced the violent disintegration of our own version of that social unit.

Glad had no experience of such work, but she set about chopping and cleaving the carcases of pigs and cows with great dexterity. She would tear the kidneys out of the ogival cavity of a lamb, the suet-encased chestnut bulb which came away with a rasping sound. She could divide a sheep's head with a single blow from a cleaver, and skinned rabbits with the ease of someone undressing a child. She handled without flinching the long tongues of chocolate-coloured liver, rubbery corrugations of tripe, the pale sphere of the heart of dead animals. Nothing could have been further from her idea of herself than her mastery of the art of butchery. She discovered a competence for which she would previously have expressed only revulsion; and the array of knives, cleavers and saws became the instruments of a livelihood she had never anticipated. Her economic survival depended no more upon choice or inclination than that of the previous generations of boot and shoe-workers, people who had moved directly from school to factory, sometimes without even a day's holiday between the two. Later, my mother showed me the savings book in which the first week's profit from the shop was recorded. It was four shillings and sixpence.

Glad loved reading. In the evenings when the shop was shut, she and Sid sat in the living-room, and she offered to read to him, recalling her popularity in the sewing class. He submitted to her enthusiasm at first, although he preferred the more excitable distraction of the radio. She took her favourite novel of the time, Grace Livingston Hill's *Coming Through the Rye*, an uplifting tale of the moral triumph of love. 'You'll like this.' When she had been reading for ten or fifteen minutes, in her clear contralto voice, she glanced up to see how he was enjoying it. He had fallen asleep. Feeling the first icy intimation of other desertions, she shivered, closed the book and rattled the poker in the scarlet embers of the dying fire. She would never read to him again, apart from occasional official letters written in a bureaucratic style he found hard to understand.

It soon became clear that Sid had no inclination for shop work. His wife had the gift of listening to customers; as she concentrated on cutting rose-coloured lamb chops or passing the rough cuts of beef through the big metal mincer, she appeared sufficiently absorbed in her work to pay only cursory attention to their stories, and they could tell her anything; in reality she was profoundly attentive. Sid had no time to listen to old wives' tales, although he was open to some of the more diverting stories of young ones; when he was serving, custom dwindled noticeably. It was not long before his function was reduced to lifting and carrying the sides of beef and pork that were delivered from the wholesaler every Tuesday. I did see him one day standing in the fridge, between sides of maroon beef hanging from steel gibbets, while the cold air rose from the silver pipes that frosted its polar interior. She jokingly made as if to close the door on him, and threatened to sell the choicest cuts of his body as a supplement to the meagre rations allowed each registered customer.

They agreed it would be better if he found a job. There was not really enough work in the shop for two people. Their income would increase and they could think about children when they had achieved a certain level of security.

He bought a lorry, and was soon carrying loads of bricks from the Bedford brickfields, staffed largely by former Italian prisoners of war. He took timber from nearby conifer plantations, manufactured metal goods from Coventry and Birmingham to distributors. He was relieved to escape the confinement of the shop, a life with few diversions from earning a living and visiting the families of her brothers and sisters. He liked none of them; Lill, fan of melodrama at the local theatre, drinker and gambler on the horses was an emissary of the future, a prototype of the later consumer, who kept Alec,

The Uses Of Adversity

her gaunt, inoffensive husband, at the household chores she disdained; Laura, 'cheerful as an epitaph' emblem of misery, whose husband Bill recounted the horrors he had seen in the First War with appalling and graphic vivacity; May, whose husband Arthur could find nothing kind to say about any foreigner, to whom he referred in a disturbing litany of monosyllables – Wops, Chinks, Japs, Cyps, Nigs and Frogs – and of whom his wife said if she had to choose between a noose and marriage to him, a noose would have been the easier way out; studious and earnest Dick, whose wife complained that he knew everything that happened two thousand years ago but didn't have a clue about what was going in the street today; Harry, who had saved up in the Post Office with Flo for twenty years to get married, and when she suggested they look at their balance, found nothing, because not only had he deposited nothing, but had regularly withdrawn everything she had contributed each week.

So the lorry, a snub-nosed vehicle which he parked beside the house in the brief intervals when he was at home, became his deliverance from responsibility. He derived great pleasure from driving the trunk roads of the Midlands late at night, while the soft bodies of moths and night creatures splashed against the windscreen, and the headlights sought out the unwinking eyes of foxes or stoats in the hedgerows. His long hours, the irregularity of the work justified lengthening absences. There was a jarring asymmetry between his physical restlessness, which found solace in continuous movement, and her inner turbulence that required the anchor of home. When they were together, their ardent incompatibilites clashed.

Sid also carried another kind of cargo, women he met on his travels, whom he found in pubs, parks and night-time streets. He would stop the truck in a lay-by, where, concealed beneath the sheet of tarpaulin with which he protected the goods he conveyed to their destination, they were secure against detection. Most of these encounters were fleeting. Occasionally they developed into a longer association, as with Pearl, with whose policeman husband Sid had an understanding; since the price he paid for access to the wife was a significant cut of some of the merchandise that fell of the back of his vehicle.

XV

At that time, the mid 1930s, our mother spent many wearying hours waiting for Sid to come home. She watched the clock, moving from room to room, cleaning the floor of the shop once more, boiling sheets in the copper, sweeping the dust and dead leaves from the garden. She prepared the orders for the following day, so that the lights shone out onto the dark road until nine thirty or ten at night. Sometimes she became angry, and no longer tried to keep his dinner appetising, but let it burn up in the oven; then, overcome by remorse, would throw it out and make something fresh. The sound of the tyres on the gravel filled her with such relief, that she would run to the door to open it for him, fill the kettle with water, place his comfortable shoes where he could step into them. None of these services placated him; he was always morose and irritable when he came home.

She hated separations; every goodbye for her foreshadowed more definitive separations. She found it difficult to live at the level of the everyday, since at every turn she saw symbols of the brevity of life, reminders of decay and loss. This filled her with strange intensities, which frightened those who never thought of suffering or mortality until these things were forcefully borne in upon them. Glad anticipated every disaster that might befall, and a good many that never would, including, of course, that which overtook her in the end.

With time, the security of always being at home yielded to the

The Uses Of Adversity

greater insecurity of those whose destiny it is to wait. My mother foresaw the risk of desertion, abandonment by him whose business took him on errands where he constantly met new people and was open to excitements she could not match. She had little to tell him, she who had learned so much about the lives of others, their shameful secrets, their illicit desires, their deceptions and disappointments. She could not broach such unwelcome topics to one who displayed no interest in them. And yet, whenever he came home, she would celebrate his arrival as though they were being reunited after a long absence; an absence which, she reasoned, he could, if he chose, have prolonged; when he had elected to come home to her.

Her eagerness evoked little response from him. He was tense from the long journey, his eyes still fixed on the long ribbon of road illuminated by the headlights. He had had a puncture. He had seen an accident. Irritation overtook him as soon as he reached home. He didn't want to talk. What else happened? Nothing. What about the accident? What accident? The one you saw. 'A man knocked off his bike. An ambulance. A red blanket. A face in pain. It happens all the time.'

She was herself full of news, but he didn't want to hear it. He was too busy with his own life to worry about anybody else's. Everything she had to tell him became entangled, and she fell silent and picked up her book. But she could not read. She would look up shyly from time to time, and if he looked at her, smile. Then he would scowl and turn away, unreachable. She knew that he could not follow her thoughts and ideas. She was ready to abandon them, unwilling to allow her intelligence to come between them. So she deliberately refrained from the exercise of her intellectual power in his company, so that he would not feel inferior. But he was also closed against her feelings; while his emotions, whatever path they might take, were fugitive and eluded her.

She thought about him obsessively. The contours of his body,

Jeremy Seabrook

the thickness of his thighs, the herringbone of dark hair from his stomach to his groin, the fragrant tufts that sprang from under his arms, the acorn of the top of his penis in repose. Sometimes, cutting the meat, she would be thinking of him, and the knife would split, cutting her finger, so that her own blood mingled with the dark trickle that came from the beef.

With time, his comings and goings became more erratic. He gave laconic accounts of his movements - a load of wood, a delivery of sacks of potatoes or coal, some bricks urgently required on site. If she asked where he was going, he replied with the evasive generalities with which the curiosity of children was checked – 'two fields the other side China' or 'to see a man about a dog.' Patronised, insulted, at length, she was so tired from her day's work, and from the mental exhaustion that came from worrying, that she no longer waited up for him. He had left part of himself elsewhere, as though the lorry-loads of stuff were only material symbols of something less tangible, but more essential. There was an absence even when he was at home, a remoteness which she did not care to define. She rehearsed all the excuses that women know, know instinctively, know by heart, even though they may never have heard them spoken. You can't expect men to care in the way women do. They can't show their feelings. They have their own rhythms that are not ours. There arose a profusion of alibis and extenuations, of a kind men never trouble to invent when they want to account for the (to them) incomprehensible ways of women.

Until that time, Glad had always felt secure behind the counter in the shop. The counter, chopping-block, a place for display and transaction, for serving, for administration of the austere diminution of the weekly meat-ration, had given her an unassailable position, from which she could listen sympathetically to the secrets and confessions of her customers. She was herself on show. She had a clear function. She was always there, discreet and attentive. Women sensed that anything they told her would go no further; they saw in

The Uses Of Adversity

her a burial-ground for secrets.

She was at first gratified by the stories women brought to her of infidelity, unhappiness or grief. Each confidence was the result of a catastrophe that had happened to another, which she had therefore been spared. One woman's husband had stolen some female underwear from a washing line. Why would he do a thing like that? his wife asked anxiously. He was a normal man. He worked on a building site. Why would he take women's slips and panties like that? She had found them crumpled beneath the mattress. 'At first, I thought they belonged to another woman. Well, they did, but not quite in the way I thought.' Later, he was actually seen unpegging the garments in the green January twilight, and followed home by the woman's husband; was caught red-handed with an underskirt and a pair of knickers concealed in his overalls. This is a matter for the police, the man who had apprehended him said grimly. 'What is it Glad?' Why would he do a thing like that? If it was another woman, I could understand it. But other women's clothes. Does he want to wear them? Does it mean he wants to be a woman? He's always been normal that way, you know.'

Glad listened solemnly. 'No', she said finally, 'it's an illness. He can't help it. He needs some sort of treatment. It's no good taking him to court over a thing like that. If they put him in prison, who will be any better off?' She was sympathetic to irregularities in the lives of people which did not affect hers; like any colonising entity, it was only for domestic purposes that she deployed her inflexible puritanical code. She was harsh upon herself, and upon those who shared her life; but did not inflict those severities on strangers.

The man did go to court. His name was published in the local paper, which served as a slightly more civilised refinement of the pillory, since it exposed the shame of wrongdoers to the community. He received letters from well-wishers, advising his family to leave the estate if they knew what was good for them. They did leave. The woman told my mother 'You're the only friend I've had.

I shall never forget you.' 'Yes, well, you know where to find me of you want me.' She felt herself out of harm's way, untouched by such afflictions.

Another woman confided in her that her husband, instead of making love to her on her wedding night, had beaten her up. It was a nightmare, she said, clenching her hands around the parcel of meat so tightly that the blood came through the newspaper. 'He turned directly after the ceremony. We went to the hotel, had a meal. He drank a bit and started sneering at me. I was scared. I thought I'd married a stranger.' 'We all marry strangers.' 'When we got to the room he started on me. He slapped me and pulled my hair. He said I wasn't a virgin. I tried to be affectionate, but it only made him more angry. I said 'I've never been with a man.' 'Who have you been with then, women?' Why does he hate me?' Her eyes filled with tears. Glad leaned over the counter and said 'He might be impotent. Had you thought of that?' 'Oh.' 'Why would he behave like that otherwise? He was scared, so he had to accuse you first. 'I thought it was me.' 'Yes, women always do. It's him, make no mistake.'

How did she know? Perhaps she had learned from her long hours of lonely conjecture during Sid's wanderings, perhaps she had glimpsed sorrows which she still believed she would be spared. Her sense of destiny fortified her against the idea that such things could happen to her; as though exemptions from the contradictions and betrayals of our troubled searchings in the bodies and souls of others were granted to anyone!

PART TWO

I

Her fears were at first concentrated on the possibility of an accident. He might die in the unsafe lorry, careering recklessly through the narrow night-time side roads. She saw the vehicle swerve as his eyelids closed with fatigue; splinters of glass and crumpled metal against a tree. She imagined Sid's body pierced by metal, bone visible through flesh. These images were so vivid she tensed herself, half-expecting the call from the police, the telephone bell, an urgent knocking at the side-door.

Her mind was drawn to other possible calamities. Hardingstone, the neat sandstone village to which she had walked over the fields as a child, had been the site of a particularly gruesome murder only a few years earlier. Known locally as the burning car murder, the victim had never been identified. Once, when my brother and I were young, we had been to see the grave, marked with a plain wooden cross and marked 'To the memory of an Unknown Man'. We were deeply affected by this austere inscription. The murderer had taken out insurance on his own life, had picked up a stranger, a hitch-hiker, and killed him. He had set fire to the car, hoping the body would be identified as his, leaving his woman-friend to claim the money from the insurance. The victim remained unnamed. No one claimed him, no one missed him. To the people of Northampton, anchored, rooted, belonging, to be without identity appeared a fate cruel beyond imagination.

Whenever Sid failed to appear, her mind ran on such implausible occurrences. She later admitted that her terror of leaving home came from this over-vivid apprehension of the worst that might happen, her ability to conceive of every possible disaster, as well as many never previously recorded in this equable land, including earthquakes and tidal waves. If she walked down the street, a car would mount the pavement and kill her. If she went abroad on holiday, some rare tropical disease would single her out and bring her down. Nor were these fears solely on her own account. When I went to India for the first time, she begged me not to go. She had foreseen a plane crash, she imagined me convulsed with typhoid or dying of malaria on the streets of Bombay. Much of this I thought was metaphor, the fear of surrendering control, expressing the intensity of her desire to hold on; if she were to let go, the whole world would be convulsed in flames. The imagery of her terrors was an emanation of the violence within, a violence not of illness or accident, but of the furious ferment of energy and emotion that had to be contained, since at that time, in that town, there was no vehicle, licensed as it were, to bear such burdens. It is not surprising that the urge to create and to act in the world, and the denial of it, led to what was later diagnosed as 'depression'. The unquiet composure was brought about by conflicting impulses within; motionlessness and melancholy were the consequence of this paralysis of the spirit.

When he didn't come home, she would walk at night through the house and shop. Whenever there was a thunderstorm, she would take down the steel choppers and knives from the rail from which they hung and conceal them so they would not attract the lightning which filled the white tiled shop with its radiance. She would sit down, stir the embers of the fire, and wonder at the signs and portents her mother had taught her to read in them – coffins and cradles according to the shape of the cinders, strangers expected when the soot flaked from the chimney, the likelihood of

The Uses Of Adversity

frost from the blue colour of the flame, while sparks flying up the chimney were souls going to heaven. Her memory was the last resting-place for much ancient lore and popular belief that died with her, the long oral memory of the life of countrypeople, which her family had been until her mother and father travelled by carrier's cart in the 1880s from Long Buckby to the unreliable shelter of rented houses in the in what people called the 'burrrows' of Northampton.

She more rarely opened a book; and if she did, her eyes scarcely registered what was printed on the page, but were fixed on the scenes of their life together; only four or five years, but already changed from the day when she stood in the backyard of her mother's house in her cloche hat, behind a bunch of white roses, and Sid's dark hair had shone like satin, and her arm rested trustingly in his. She sometimes took out that photograph, as though by looking at it she could trace the feelings that had dissolved so swiftly since that bright July day when she had smiled her pallid smile, framed by the zinc bath on its rusty nail in the brickwork, and next door's cat basked in the sunlight on the wall, the shadows soon to overtake it still an insignificant oblong on the brick path.

She knew that the intensity of relationships cannot be sustained and must cool with time; otherwise, you would never be able to get on with your life, work would be neglected and the demands of the world go unheeded. For the first year and a half, Sid had not objected to her obsession with him. On the contrary, he was flattered, since it made him feel, briefly, safe; secure against the persistence of desire which flickered like fire in him, and risked flaring up wherever combustible material was to be found. He perhaps also believed Glad might rescue him from whatever it was he most feared within. In the beginning, they had been overtaken by urgencies that would not be denied. They once even shut the shop on a Saturday afternoon, busiest day of the week, and customers had angrily rattled the shop door, while they giggled upstairs at their own wanton daring.

Glad had always been alert to any diminution in his response to her. She loved to feel his movement inside her, and never failed to wonder at her ability to create an arousal in him swift and total. She was not sure about her own enjoyment: was it because of what seemed like her power over him, or was it more spontaneous and unreflecting? Glad always had a strong sense of sexual inferiority, had never considered herself desirable. Was his desire for her a result of his inability to reach her intelligence, a need to subordinate this, to bring it down to something in which he could express his supremacy? Whatever the cause, as long as they continued in happy misapprehension of one another, everything went well.

It was perhaps inevitable that her relationships would be obsessive. She poured into her husband all the choked impulses and smothered exaltations of her mind and spirit, He was the only object of her narrow but profound intensity; and it was bound to become onerous to him, as it was to chafe at the constraints it imposed upon her.

If none of her sisters had ever mentioned their sexual experience with anything like enthusiasm, this resignation was echoed by the women on the estate. They would come into the shop on Monday mornings, raise their eyes in a mute appeal to a heaven from which they expected no succour, and complained they were black and blue from their weekend mauling. Expecting little, they were rarely disappointed. They often said they lived only for their children. If it were not for them, they would walk out on him tomorrow. This was also only a figure of speech, for although walking was the only form of movement they had access to, it promised no destination of deliverance.

In the early days, even the smallest drift of his attention from her had made her unhappy, close to despair, since even this modest cooling seemed to presage the end. She exhausted herself trying to recapture his interest. Soon after their marriage, if he failed stiffen

The Uses Of Adversity

as he lay beside her, she panicked, imagining at once that their relationship was finished. If, in the beginning, she had underestimated the capacity for renewal of the reservoir of desire, she later failed to perceive the quickening of a real estrangement; and it was not until the distance between them had become unbridgeable that she realised that when desire dies, it ebbs unobtrusively, and becomes visible only through its absence.

Suddenly, and without warning, he became less irritable, more conciliatory. Perhaps this meant a halt to the downward slide of indifference. Perhaps this was the way things were. Relationships stabilise in a more or less affectionate acceptance of the way things are. She sought comfort in her clever woman's rationalising. But it didn't work. She could not fail to observe that he was taking care to make the best of himself whenever he said he was going 'out for a drink', that apparently most guileless of male outings. In the look he gave himself as he moistened his hair with lard, she could see the appraisal of the woman he was to meet. Sid had never had friends. He had enjoyed the company of what Glad disparagingly referred to as 'pals', relationships which implied both superficiality and exploitation, They were mainly people with whom he was going to conduct business deals; which meant, for the most part, lending them money. He was going into the timber business, and installed a saw-bench and engine at the bottom of the garden. For a few days the rotating blade ate into a load of timber, emitting a shower of wooden sparks. The apparatus soon fell into rust and was dismantled, sold for scrap by another of his associates. He was going to earn money from keeping fowls. But the hen run was neglected and produced swarms of rats; they had to get a neighbour's dog to destroy them; in any case, the hens became diseased and died. He concluded drunken deals with solemn pledges which he failed to remember the following day, even though the partners, equally drunk, rarely did so, and presented themselves, aggrieved and demanding that Glad honour promises Sid had made – a loan of a hundred pounds, an investment here, some small capital outlay there. He showed a childish delight in new things, but had little capacity for sustained effort; and he cast each new craze aside; he was once told by a fortune teller that he would 'come into money', and blamed his wife, with her long face and her temper that would never go mouldy with keeping, for the ruin of the promised good luck.

When she could no longer hide from herself the extent of his disengagement from her, she told herself she was being morbid, unreasonable. She had inherited the lugubrious sensibility of her mother's family, which was partly a secular residue of decayed religious fervour, and partly a quite practical determination to be prepared for the worst, which rarely delayed long in their experience of poverty and misfortune. It caused my mother to spend so much time contemplating an eternity she considered unlikely, that she failed to avail herself of the delights of this world. The old aunts liked nothing better than to sit in the churchyard, where they knew the inscriptions on the gravestones by heart and contemplated an afterlife they did not doubt would come. As long as this melancholy attached itself to a religious tradition, it was cathartic. Only when all sacred associations had fallen away, it appeared as an individual affliction, a derangement of the spirit.

She saw in memory all the places they had visited together, transformed at the time by the intensity of her feeling for him. The clearings in the forest had never been so drenched in sunlight; the red campion had never been so vivid, the ladysmocks never smelled so sweet, the buttercups had never shone as they did that May. She told herself that people remain faithful to each other because they are grateful for the changes in perception of the world which the other person has helped bring about. You feel you have been loved, and that makes for commitment and duty beyond desire. Love becomes a milder recognition, a more durable commitment, unshakeable affection. The appetites abate as the years pass. You can-

The Uses Of Adversity

not recapture it, because the way in which it alters you and your relationship to everything around you, can, by its nature, occur only once. To have been loved is to have been transformed. That is surely enough.

My mother knew that she was capable of responding to other men. In the shop, enough men had given her the glad eye for her to realise that her youthful vigour and animation made of her a not unattractive woman, despite her self-doubt. She wondered if there was something in the sight of a woman laying about herself with an axe, performing a labour of butchery, male labour, that might arouse certain men. But she wouldn't be so foolish. Her own feelings for Sid were so powerful, she almost believed that they could not, by a kind of sympathetic magic, fail to evoke a similar response in him. She projected her own intensities onto him and did her best to read in them his answering mood.

On the increasingly rare evenings when he was at home, they sat on opposite sides of the fireplace, and he would escape her watchfulness by flight into sleep, or a pretence of it. He closed his eyes to avoid her searching regard. But she couldn't help herself. She would sigh, turn away, make as if to read. She could no longer concentrate. Words on the page that had once been so enthralling now ceased to move her. She had learned much from what she read; so much indeed, that she had to feign ignorance, so as not to express, however inadvertently, in his presence, her superior understanding. There was, it sometimes seemed, no limit to the violence she did to herself in order to accommodate him. She unlearned all that she had taken from the novels of the nineteenth century – George Eliot, Mrs Gaskell, Dickens and Thackeray. She had to do so if she was to pretend to herself that all she had read was only fiction, and that real people could behave as Sid behaved, and still love her.

He accused her of being possessive. She had always been jealous. Because of her position as youngest in the family, she felt she was an afterthought, having come so late into a world already so old and fully populated with brothers and sisters – her oldest sister was already married when she was born. She had to struggle for recognition. All the affections of the family had already been distributed in an emotional space no more commodious than that of the cramped rented houses where they lived. She had arrived in an already occupied country. She felt she had prowled around the already complete entity of a family, looking for a point of entry; the more so since after her, no one else came. It left her with a need to distinguish herself, and especially to be loved without threat or rival.

There are some things we desperately try to avoid telling ourselves, for once spoken, we never cease to repeat them. She told herself at last that he must have found someone else, not the fly-by-night wenches who had been seen (where?) to climb down from the back of his truck in the middle of the night, covered in brick-dust or with wood-shavings in their hair. She looked at her body in the wardrobe mirror and tried to imagine what qualities any new love might require. It couldn't be intelligence, but then it wasn't intelligence he was looking for when he met Glad: what he liked was the idea of vanquishing intelligence; in which, she concluded with regret, he had been very successful. The distinction of being clever was no longer a consolation to her. She longed to be beautiful, with a fierce resentful yearning; and so desperately that sometimes she behaved as though it were true, and held herself in a way that she had seen people of great physical perfection do, looking neither to right nor left, secure in the looks of envy, admiration or desire that followed them wherever they went. Then she would catch sight of her prominent nose in the glass of the scales in the shop, or see her reflection in the darkening night window, and she shrank to the plain undistinguished figure she was, hunched, apologetic. How little, she thought, we value the qualities we have, in what small regard we hold them; and how we covet the attributes of others,

The Uses Of Adversity

even though those who have them are rarely made conspicuously happier by their possession.

She might have been comforted to know that Sid was not preoccupied with one woman, but with women, all women. He was infinitely distractible, a condition from which he had hoped, in vain, that Glad would rescue him. A woman had only to appear to smile at him in the street, and he would follow her, in order to discover the meaning of her glance. He was frequently confronted by an indignant stranger, who asked him how he dared to follow her, and who threatened to call the police if he didn't leave her alone. But often, enchanted by the charm of his address, they did not repel him, His erratic comings and goings, the faulty delivery of goods – often to the wrong destination – the missed appointments, were not so much a criticism of his wife as a symptom of his own disorder; but any consolation this knowledge might have brought was denied her; and she continued to succumb to feelings of inadequacy and rejection; feelings which, however painful, had at least an aspect of familiarity. Sometimes, it seems, we organise the world around us in such a way that it yields, not the fulfilment or happiness we think we are looking for, but the deeper affirmation that we really are as we suspect, and merit only disappointment and negation..

It seemed to her she would never enjoy the distinction of his unshared affection. She had made such efforts to overcome the disadvantages of poverty – by reading, by changing her accent, so that she no longer spoke with the raw regional accent, but had acquired a neutral English which made some people call her 'stuck-up'. She had tried to cultivate qualities that would make her remarkable, and by means of which she could obtain what her natural physical endowments could never guarantee. While she waited for Sid to come home, she quoted Shakespeare, Shelley, Wordsworth to herself, but these were poor companions now. While she waited, she longed for him to come back, on any terms. But as soon as he came in, she could sense the ghostly presence of whoever he had been with, and who had drawn him away from her. Immensely impressionable, Sid always bore, as it were, the traces of those he had just left. When he looked at her, she saw in his eyes the cruellest of all questions, why are you not someone else? That she had failed him was the unspoken assumption; that he might have failed her, repeatedly, without compunction, did not seem to occur to him.

I was reminded, when she told me this towards the end of her life, of a friend of mine, an actor, who died in her late thirties. She was living in Canada, working in the theatre, and learned she had inoperable cancer only two weeks before she died. She left two young children. She spent the few days remaining to her preparing for her death and organising what remained of her life as best she could. When I heard that she had died, I went to visit her mother in Northampton. The woman said How kind of you to visit; but as she looked at me her eyes said, Why my beautiful daughter with her young children, and why not you. There was in her gaze a naked resentment that no words could tell. I could never bear to see her again.

My mother was not embittered by her life with Sid, at least not yet, but it made her sadder, and reinforced her melancholy. Perhaps that is what experience does: it brings a more ready unfolding of who we are, which we sometimes call wisdom.

II

Sometimes when I went to see her in the home, she would look at me between arthritic fingers splayed at the side of her face, and say 'I hate every minute of it.' She spoke with great vehemence, and I knew exactly what she felt, since I also have experienced time as though it were an alien element, to be alternately battled against

The Uses Of Adversity

and endured. I know her story, not only because she narrated it – which she did sparingly – but because I was inhabited by the same sensibility, the spirit that was hers; I was going to say 'possessed', because that is how it sometimes felt. There is no fault or culpability in this, an impersonal inheritance that flowed through the family for generations, a sombre anticipation of tragedy and loss; and although this took little account of the joys and delight in life, they were more often than not accurate in their anticipation of woes to come.

When she said she hated every minute, she meant she was never at ease with life. Time, which passes so swiftly and unnoticed, had caught her up in what seem to her its alien compulsion, which made everything onerous to her. Her life was always led in past or future, because the moment was usually unbearable; so damaged by fears of the future or haunted by the events of the past, even its pleasures; for pleasures themselves had not been at all agreeable at the time, but could be savoured only once they had been safely negotiated, and were finally free of contamination by a dangerous and unreliable present. The present was hostile territory to be crossed, even though the future offered no real sanctuary, particularly as she grew older. The greatest benefit of the future occurred while it still contained the adults her sons would become, and the certainty that we would look after her. The past became the place where she spent most of her time; not, of course, a real past, because it had been too cruel then, but a past from which she had emerged safely if not unscarred, and which was now beyond impairment or loss. As she aged, she said that her happiest times were when we were small children, still dependent upon her, tractable and replete with the promise of a future not yet spoiled by its realisation. With her, I understood the roots of nostalgia, that celebration of the irrecoverable; celebration because we have lived to tell the tale. Nostalgia is a festival for survivors.

When I was with my mother, I was aware of a kinship of sensi-

61

bility which can exist independently of blood-relationships. I thought of George Eliot, who had written that Nature was a great tragic dramatist, binding people together by flesh and bone, yet dividing them by more subtle differences of temper and sensibility which jar at every moment. Possibly even more tragic was the condition of my mother and me, united by sensibility but separated by gender and generation.

I was attached to her by the consciousness of an identical, but often burdensome, predicament. She never needed to explain things to me, which perhaps accounted for the fullness of the silences between us. A common apprehension of the world made all the stories and gossip I saved up to tell her diversions from the reluctant communion between us. When I now remember the hours I passed in her company, so many of them were speechless, a dumb amazement that the boundaries of self were so fluid and indeterminate. I felt porous and ghost-like. She inhabited us both.

She could perhaps contemplate with serenity the perpetuation of her melancholy existence in me, a kind of provisional immortality. She was more like my real twin than my brother. He remained inaccessible to us both, estranged by a personality that neither she nor I understood. In this lay the origin of the bitterness he was to feel against us, although what I shared with my mother was no consolation either. My brother, distant and mysterious, fascinated her a great deal more than I did. She preferred him to me (I suspect I did also), although this never appeared so to him, who took the unsought, and often unwelcome, union between us for a conspiracy against him. He dealt with it in his own way; a loneliness which made him appear aloof; and he responded to this, in the end, by severing all connection with both of us.

When she referred to herself, waiting for Sid to come home, straining to hear the sound of the lorry, his key in the lock, I immediately knew the agitation and conflicting feelings she must have known; for I, too, seem to have been waiting all my life for people

The Uses Of Adversity

to arrive; for my mother to come to bed when I was a child; for friends who promised to call when I was an adolescent; for my partner to come home as an adult. I have also been constantly expectant and unsettled, listening for the phone, waiting for the post, expecting an e-mail, wondering if I had missed the urgent message that might transform my life. I did not need to imagine her impatience and disappointment, as she invented things to do in the spaces between waiting and homecoming.

III

I have in front of me a piece of thin paper, dated 12th February 1952, with the heading in Gothic lettering, **In the High Court of Justice**. Beneath are the words Probate, Divorce and Admiralty Division (what had the Admiralty to do with the ending of marriages? Burial at sea?) (DIVORCE) at Northampton District Registry. Beneath, there is a list – Petitioner, Respondent, Co-Respondent. My mother is named as the Petitioner and her husband the Respondent. No Co-Respondent is named.

It goes on 'Referring to the decree made in this Cause on the 12th day of February 1952, whereby it was decreed that the marriage had and (sic) solemnized on the 2nd day of June 1930, at the Parish Church of S. Edmund Northampton in the County of Northampton between Gladys Annie Seabrook, then Youl (spinster) the Petitioner, and Sydney Robinson Seabrook the Respondent be dissolved by reason that since the celebration thereof the said Respondent had deserted the Petitioner without cause for a period of at least three years immediately preceeding (sic) the presentation of the Petition unless sufficient cause be shown to the Court within six weeks from the making thereof why the said Decree should not be made absolute and no such cause having been shown, it is hereby certified that the said Decree was on the 1st day of April 1952, made final and absolute and that the said Marriage was thereby dissolved.'

If it had not been already dissolved, it surely would have done so in the corrosive acid of a biting bureaucratic indifference of language, with its inflated and careless wording. Seldom can official records contain as many fictions as this scrap of paper from a time of true austerity (it measures about 20cms by 25cms). It also conceals a depth of misery endured by my mother which few women would now tolerate.

We were twelve at the time. Her anxiety over the proceedings affected her, my brother and me for weeks beforehand. On the day of the court hearing, which she was obliged to attend in person, she left us with her sister. Although it was April, she took us to a still wintry park, where rust had corroded the municipal green paint of the swings, and their metal chains squealed as they chafed the frame which supported them. The chill melancholy of separation had penetrated our leather helmets and hand-knitted mittens and we took little pleasure in the deserted playground. We waited restlessly for her to collect us, Our aunt had bought some pieces of confectionery, vanilla slices, a small compensation for what she regarded as our semi-orphaned condition.

It was late afternoon when our mother arrived. She was flushed and her eyes shone with a fierce light. She took us firmly by the hand and we walked to the bus station, facing the cold wind of her lonely status as divorced woman. After she died, I found among her papers a testimonial to the court from one of her customers, prominent owner of a perambulator and toy store in the town. It reads 'Sirs, I have known Mrs Seabrook over fifteen years and have always found her honest, truthful and most conscientious and a person of the highest character.' This represented an authority that could be expected to count against her husband's complaint that he had been driven away by constant 'nagging'; a term much used by

The Uses Of Adversity

men at that time to allay their own guilt and extenuate their infidelities.

I remember the trepidation with which each evening in the steely twilight of that early April she opened the Chronicle and Echo, our local newspaper, dreading the appearance of her name. And one day, there it was. Decrees Absolute. There were only three or four, but virtually everyone in Northampton took the paper, precisely for reasons such as this, to keep track of the lives of acquaintances, work-mates and neighbours; not only their weddings and deaths, but also news of those who had proved too weak to sustain without complaint the expected injuries of marriage.

The attribution of the cause of breakdown to mere desertion provided some faint relief to my mother, since no Co-respondent had been named. The neighbours did not necessarily see this as a mitigating circumstance, since some assumed she was possessed of repelling characteristics that had driven her husband away, or worse, was of such meagre allure (her own conviction) that she failed to hold him. In any case, she was the sole occupant of a butcher's shop at the time, and a significant number of customers – particularly those from the better-off parts of the estate – came to withdraw their ration-books from her custody, since although they had no objection to a woman running a shop, they could scarcely be expected to countenance breaches of marriage vows, those strenuous ligatures designed to stem the flow of desire. Others, less sophisticated, also withheld their custom, but for more archaic reasons, namely, that meat handled by a menstruating woman would surely go bad.

Social humiliation was not the smallest part of the price of divorce. She was marked. The role of 'divorced woman' brought with it, not only the suspicion of other women, but also unwanted attentions from their husbands who, instructed by Hollywood in the nature of divorcees, believed she might offer the chance for a bit of extra-marital fun. They must have been puzzled by her response, since she probably told them, in an earthy homage to her roots, that they could piss their tallow where they pissed their beer.

Set against the eighteen year ordeal of her marriage, shame seemed a relatively painless cost. Within a few months, she had sold the shop, paid off the remaining mortgage and taken us to live with her sister, Aunt Em, who had a reputation for saintliness unmatched by anyone else in the family. Sid had not contested her right to the proceeds from a labour he had long abandoned, since he enjoyed lucrative contracts with firms whose goods he transported, as well as the advantages of being a pioneer of that picaresque hero, the trucker; his purposeful mobility must have been a powerful aphrodisiac to the place-bound women who hitched lifts with him to fabulous destinations in Coventry and Leicester.

The taint of divorce followed my mother. Once your name had been 'in the paper', it would be remembered in perpetuity. The memory of women who were, on the whole, kept without intellectual occupation, was a vast repository of information, a filing-system of extraordinary range and cross-reference, which would have been the envy of any totalitarian bureaucracy, since all information, unlike that of the unforgiving archive of political control, could be retrieved at a moment's notice.

IV

Gladys in her late sixties became afraid to leave the house. There had been an accident in the store where she and her sister would hunt for bargains; one of the austere pleasures of people who, brought up poor, take pleasure in buying some unnecessary article for next to nothing – a new tea-towel, a cardigan, a box of handkerchiefs. This was as close as my mother came to extravagance. A boy on a skateboard had been riding the wooden-floor of the old-

The Uses Of Adversity

fashioned shop, and he crashed into her, slightly damaging her foot. What, her sisters asked one another, were children doing on skateboards in shops? But then, what were children doing anyway, listening to music, eating chicken out of a red-and-white striped box, or dripping the liquid from melting ice lollies onto racks of garments? The incident was not serious. The boy apologised profusely; but it undermined her already shaken confidence. After that, she rarely left the house, and in retrospect, she magnified the extent of her injury. It became an emblem of the dangers that lay in wait beyond the familiar confines of the house.

Her outings had already been reduced to the half-mile walk from the house into the centre of town; an itinerary she followed almost every week-day for twenty five years. Apparently eventless, it was packed with significance for her – meetings with people she knew, encounters never planned but renewed each week, contact with people lost sight of. She returned full of news after each modest expedition – who she had run into, who looked like death warmed up, whose shed had been broken into, whose cat ran up whose entry, as they used to say of the involuntary intimacies of neighbourly closeness. Her walk took her down the red funnel of the street, built soon after the death of the tenacious Lord Palmerston, after whom it was called. She went past the coach-house that belonged to a huge layer-cake yellow and red Gothic fantasy which had once been the home of a shoe manufacturer, but had become offices of the Regional Health Authority, all strip-lighting and gunmetal filing cabinets where once the daughters of plutocrats had danced till dawn while their suitors drank champagne from their slipper; along the main road where, among the villas mostly diverted to commercial activity, there lingered an imperious widow behind tasselled velvet and a magnolia tree with blooms white as wax. She might make a short detour to pass by the allotments, where rose-coloured drifts of fruit blossom gathered beside the wooden fence or the miniature lanterns of raspberries glowed red among wet leaves. There, she sometimes met an old man who declared he was 'sweet on her', and to prove it, sometimes came to our house with gifts of blue savoy cabbage, sticks of fleshy rhubarb or onions in papery skins. From there, she passed through the churchyard, where the boot and shoe masters lay in competitively ornate splendour and the sorrow of their widows was measured in wrought iron and weathered angels with empty eyes. She would pause at the library where, under the death-mask of John Clare, elderly women fought one another for possession of love-books, stories of the amours of society hostesses, air aces and surgeons with a deft healing touch. Then on to the market square. This was always thronged with people she knew – girls she had worked with, women whose weddings she had attended, people who had lived next door at some point during their frequent removals. Clusters of people formed and dissolved on the cobbles of the market square, a spontaneous choreography of provincial life, by turns solemn and gay, as they monitored the progress of an illness, the decline of a marriage, a new birth or an unexpected legacy. They shopped on the market for fresh produce, windfallen apples, new potatoes, squeaky pea-pods, carrots still attached to their bright green plumes.

After her accident, even these familiar scenes were fraught with terror. She would not linger, even in a relative's house, but was always on edge, anxious to return home and close the door. She would sink into a chair with a cup of tea, in the reassuring company of her solitude.

Occasionally, she would sit on a bench close to the allotments. Strangers who shared the seat would sometimes ask her what was the matter. Her face, in repose, always wore an expression of such dejection that people concluded she had been abandoned that same day by a lover or husband, or had suffered a sudden bereavement. When she stood in shop queues, sat on the bus, she always looked as though she were on the point of losing the struggle against over-

The Uses Of Adversity

whelming grief. One day an old man said to her 'Cheer up duck, it may never happen.' She turned her sad gaze upon him and said 'Oh yes, duck. It already has.'

She fled to doctors to assuage illness they could not diagnose, pains without name that only illuminated for them the limits of their competence. She found relief in diazepam, nitrazepam; tranquillisers and sleeping tablets, even though by this time her life suffered from an excess of tranquillity and a surfeit of sleep. She was not without insight into her condition. She said 'The only thing wrong with me is who I am. There's only one cure for that, and that'll be when they put me to bed with a shovel.'

Later, she did find comfort in a psychiatric hospital, the grounds of which extended close to the bottom of our street. It was a private clinic, in which many wealthy and famous people found solace for their ailments; and the fact of her referral as one of the few National Health Service patients made her feel special. Behind its discreet walls expansive lawns were shaded by luxuriant copper beeches and spacious rooms were ornamented by plaster cornices of oak leaves and acorns. She was suddenly among TV stars who had attempted suicide, titled people who had nervous breakdowns, the children of celebrities addicted to drugs and drink. Some of them befriended her, telling of their wretchedness, the ruin of their gilded lives; which was possibly of greater therapeutic value to her than any formal treatment she received. She said 'Rich people tell you money doesn't bring happiness. That's only thing they say that nobody believes.'

Before this, there were frequent admissions into the general hospital, the former Northampton Infirmary, a building still regarded with misgiving when we were children, since it was believed to be the place where people went to die. But by the 1980s, it had become a refuge, where my mother felt secure. She sat cheerfully in bed, grey against the implacable whiteness of the sheets and the silver metal bedframe. Being in hospital always revived her spirits considerably. The truth was that she loved being with people when compelled into their company, but by choice, perversely, she shunned them. In hospital she became sociable and expansive, and she was often kept in beyond the strict term required by whatever ailed her – itself often obscure – because, in her uniquely perverse way, she cheered everyone else up.

V

Many older women imagine they are being robbed. They often become suspicious of an individual, perhaps one on whom they have become dependent, and accuse her of stealing from them clothing, money, even things of no value at all.

In the two or three years before my mother and Aunt Em moved to the nursing home, they were looked after by a woman in her sixties, but who, at times, appeared even more infirm than either of them. Grace smoked incessantly. She was thin and failed to eat properly, even though she had always considered it her duty to place mountains of food before the men in her family. She became very attached to the two old ladies. She arrived at the house at 7.30 to get them up and make tea. She would arrive in her thin boots, through which the damp had seeped, her sparse hair clinging to her scalp in an aureole of unmelted snow, her hands numb with cold. She was animated by a compelling, almost penitential, need to look after others, at the same time, neglecting herself. This was part of a women's work of expiation without end, a scouring and polishing, adjusting curtains, straightening carpets, setting everything in its place; a doomed and semi-religious occupation which in an age of faith would have been absorbed in accepted public ritual, but in a secular time was interpreted as an obsessive disorder.

For a time, my mother rejoiced in Grace's devotion, for it en-

The Uses Of Adversity

abled them to stay longer in their own home. After a few months, however, she began to wonder at Grace's zeal, and to doubt the disinterestedness of her concern for two old women, who were, despite the generosity of what they paid her, strangers to her. Gladys became convinced that Grace was taking things from the house. When she came in the morning, her leather shopping-bag was empty; when she left, it was bulging. My mother swore she had seen her in the kitchen, rubbing the laundry-mark from tea-towels, although by that time my mother was unable to move from her chair. She insisted that everyone who visited the house should check the wardrobe, to make sure her clothes were intact. She had a substantial cache of good quality clothes passed on by her niece; garments she had never worn and now never would; but to maintain them in a state of readiness of future events and high days she would never see, became one of her principal interests. She was certain that Grace was filching them one by one, although there was never any depletion of the store in the wardrobe which still contained her fox fur with its glassy eyes, a slim crepe de chine black dress with moons and stars appliquéd in silver and a strong smell of mothballs.

Glad was adamant that Grace was taking things. She knew it in the way people have faith; and would hear no denial or extenuation. Grace could not be trusted. One of her boys had been in court for stealing a car. If anyone said 'Why would she steal anything? She is well paid for the work she does, why would she risk that for a few old garments scarcely worth money?' my mother flew into a rage, which, because of her immobility, was even more terrifying in its captive intensity. Instead of responding, the question became one of loyalty to my mother. 'You're taking her side against me. I'm on my own. Nobody believes me. But I *know*.' Anyone who contradicted her was an enemy. In this way, she retained her sense of being special, since she was endowed with unique insight; lonely, self-absorbed, but distinguished from everyone around her, as she had always longed to be. Sometimes, exasperated by her accusations, I asked her 'How can you know what you haven't seen?' She would say 'Don't ask me. I just know.' This had been a familiar response when my brother and I were small. She gave us to understand she was granted insights not of this world. She even hinted at more sombre powers, and more than once suggested that she could 'ill-wish' people. 'I've only got to wish them harm, and something will happen'; invoking perhaps some slumbering belief in witchcraft that had smouldered in the placid countryside of Northampton-shire for generations, never quite banished either by Christian virtue or the strength of reason.

Grace knew nothing of my mother's suspicions, but gradually, Glad began to behave more coldly to the woman who had saved them from the 'home' they dreaded, and had done so far more effectively than the sons who had vowed to protect her from such a fate. My mother had originally greeted her in the morning with gratitude, her presence signalling that the long wakeful night was over. Now she barely acknowledged her.

Yet even when the old ladies were in the nursing home, Grace continued to visit, always taking some small treat she thought they might enjoy. My mother had conceived a passion for toffees called Devon Dainties, which she chewed ferociously, finally ruining the teeth she had been proud of. One day, the matron went in to Glad and said 'Grace has come to see you.' My mother said 'Well I don't want to see her. I don't want her anywhere near me.' Grace, who had been waiting behind the door, heard this. She left the bunch of pink roses she had cut from the bush in her garden and fled in tears. She never visited again. My aunt wondered what had happened to her, and asked me to go and see if she was all right. Not long after, Grace died of the cancer that was already within her when she was nursing the two old women, who both outlived her.

The refusal of anyone to support her conviction that Grace was stealing from her became another proof of Glad's belief that in the

The Uses Of Adversity

end you are on your own. It was her lesson in existential desolation, evidence that we are all deserted at last, even by those who protest their love most loudly. Her adjurations were meant for me; for she was also accusing me, saying 'You will not come with me. You too will abandon me. You will go on living when I am dead. You will not even keep me company through the losses of old age, whereas I came through everything with you. I never deserted you.' It was as though she resented the absence of some custom of *sati* whereby children immolated themselves with their dead parents.

Apart from these obsessions and the mild paranoia expressed in her stories and parables, she remained lucid. She was quite clear that this was not the onset of dementia. She had seen too many elderly whose own children had become, literally, strangers to them (not the wilful defection I was accused of), and who had been unable to remember their names. She had no intention of giving in to that kind of forgetfulness. To convince any doubters that her mind was unclouded, she would quote the long speeches of Polonius or Portia, or Grey's Elegy, enunciating the verses with great fluency, a child once more, sitting bolt upright in the straitjacket wood-and-metal desk in a chalky Edwardian schoolroom. The soundness of her memory impressed the staff, who sometimes took prospective residents to meet her, as though displaying a star pupil at an expensive school.

In extreme old age, she reverted to that most significant of times, when her purpose as mother had flooded her whole being, requiring neither reflection nor apology. She would say 'I had to be both mother and father to you'; and she had indeed shown a formidable capacity to unite features traditionally attributed to the sexual division of parental labour. She had controlled us with a powerful discipline that required no physical chastisement, and had loved us with a suffocating intensity. She had provided us with both moral instruction and entertainment. She had read to us a great deal. Sometimes in her haste to have us grow up, that she might share her life with us more fully, she sometimes misjudged our capacity for understanding. When we were about eight, she had begun *The Scarlet Pimpernel*, Baroness Orczy's heroic tales of the British aristocrat who rescued many of his French counterparts from the guillotine. When Sir Percy is escaping the bloodlust of crazed revolutionaries, with the pale slender-throated princess beneath a rough cover in his cart, he bawls out that he is driving a vehicle full of victims of smallpox; and the revolutionaries slink away. I was terrified by the mention of smallpox, which added yet another deadly disease to the lengthening list of those which I feared would remove our mother from us before we were sufficiently independent to look after ourselves, and she had to put the book aside, because the sight of it made me howl. We had sat long evenings by the fire when, in an attempt to cultivate our minds, she had permitted us to stay up beyond our bedtime to listen to some new soprano on the radio sing One Fine Day or Oh my Beloved Father. She would wash us both in the same water from a chipped enamel bowl set down on the carpet, over which she always made the sign of the cross with her finger before starting on whoever had second turn; this, she told us, was to make sure the devil didn't get us. Many ancient superstitions, some of great antiquity, which came from the country childhood of her parents, were offered up to us, partly to divert us with archaic practices, but also in some measure to pass on to us the last shreds that remained of a decayed animist faith.

She saw her life, with its frugality and self-denial, as a time of continuous dispossession. The extended network of kin among whom she had grown, was frayed; the fabric torn. The nuclear family which succeeded it fell apart even more readily; and kinsfolk became absentee relatives, whose claims were reduced to a Christmas card and a dutiful appearance at funerals. The money she had laboured to save from the shop, and which was to have provided security in her old age, was all used up in a few months on nursing home fees. Although she always professed herself a socialist, she

The Uses Of Adversity

resented her own final dependency. Even the sons, from whom many innocent and quite unrealisable vows had been elicited, promises that they would indeed look after her, who had sworn she should sit on silver and gold cushions when she grew old (did we really make such an offer spontaneously, or was it somehow prompted by her?), had apparently abandoned her to the indifferent hands of professional carers, a category of humanity she would once have found beyond comprehension.

VI

When Sid had finally departed, and the shop sold – it became a do-it-yourself store – we went to live with Aunt Em in her little terraced house in the street where Gran had also recently died. Aunt Em was a woman whose purpose in life was clearly indicated to her by events. And she never hesitated a moment in fulfilling it. Four years older than my mother, she was a good woman, in a way her sister could not claim to be.

Aunt Em's life was unstained by guilt or remorse. She married her husband in the early 1920s, when he was invalided out of the Royal Navy with TB. He had become ill, rescuing White Russian refugees escaping the Revolution, and who were taken to Novaya Zemlaya in 1917 and 18. if there was irony in Uncle Frank's counter-revolutionary rescue mission in a family, most of whom called themselves socialists, no one ever referred to it. For in 1923, he was given two years to live; and it was under this sentence of death hat Aunt Em married him. He lived a further twenty five years. She never said so, because she was modest and self-effacing, but it was undoubtedly her love that prolonged his life. He had spent a few months in a sanatorium, where the beds where wheeled at night onto a freezing verandah, since fresh air was then considered the only palliative. At his entreaty, Aunt Em had taken him home, not to die, but to thrive on her devotion. It gave her a passionate belief in the healing capacity of love, not as a sentimental theory, but in disciplined, unflagging practice over many years. Love, she said, was labour.

Uncle Frank was also a significant figure in our lives, another man to whom access was forbidden, also because of sickness; although this was of a different order from the shaming affliction that barred us from Sid. Frank's was a sickness of nobility and sacrifice, contracted in the service of the country. We rarely visited the little terraced house, where he sat in bed for many years, breathing with the fragile remains of a single lung.

The figure of the self-sacrificing woman was familiar in the streets. Many remained unmarried. They were compassionate and accepting of their fate, since their contribution was widely acknowledged by the community. Aunt Em also looked after her mother as she grew older, while her elder brother also came within the scope of her care, since he had remained at home, a characteristic male incompetent, lost if his dinner was not set in front of him when he came home from the factory for his mid-day break.

You could distinguish them in town, as they scanned the stores for some small luxury to tempt the taste of the infirm or elderly relatives for whom they bore responsibility. Often untidy, they had little concern for their appearance, and were often in a slight hurry, preoccupied with the one they had left, wondering if she might have a fall, or have wandered out of doors in her night-dress, if something terrible might not have happened during her brief absence. These women, with their choiceless self-abnegation tended the victims of industrial accidents, the man crushed by a beer barrel falling from a dray, the worker maimed by the collapse of scaffolding in a high wind, as well as the war-mutilated, elderly children only ninepence in the shilling, the emotionally broken, and the casualties of industrial life.

The Uses Of Adversity

Some remained unmarried because a fiancé died in the First World War. Our neighbour, whose betrothed was one of the last to die in 1918, had everything prepared for the wedding, and for the rest of her life, her trousseau remained, pillowcases stained with mildew, lace eaten away by sunlight and moth, china cups crisscrossed with tiny cracks, soap hardened and flaking, utensils corroded by rust in the damp spare room where her unfulfilled life lay hoarded.

These charitable women often made up a significant portion of the dwindling attendance at churches and chapels. On Sunday mornings, sedate and solitary, they made their way to places of worship, where they thanked their Maker for the privilege of serving him in the shape of his wounded creation. They had at least two consolations, which many of their successors – of whom there are many – lack. One was public recognition. Known to everyone, they were looked upon with admiration much in the way that people now regard celebrities and media heroes – they were deferred to and loved as flesh and blood, an inspiration to others to strive and to endure. Today's five million 'carers' are often seen as objects of pity, at best unfortunates, whose lives have been blighted, at worst, losers, unable to get out from the charge of duties they have been landed with.

The second great comfort was that they were rarely alone in their commitment. They were often part of a wider network, who regularly relieved them of their role. Once a week, Aunt Em visited us, knowing that her mother was sitting with Uncle Frank; another afternoon she went with her sister to the cinema, since a neighbour could be relied upon to take her husband his afternoon cup of milk. Such women were part of an invisible, tenacious mesh of humanity, which didn't call itself 'caring' because that was its clear and spontaneous purpose.

A few men also fulfilled this role. Next door to us an unmarried man lived with his elderly mother. She became more frail, her legs ulcerated and had to be amputated. He worked in a factory; and since Aunt Em was rarely absent for long, it was no hardship for her to look in each day. The son said that since his mother had cared for him when he was helpless, it was only natural that he should perform the same service for her. When people asked him when he was going to get married, he said 'My Mam is my only sweetheart'. And people didn't sniff and think of him as a timorous pouf, although by some definition he might have been. On the contrary, many women looked at him with a wistful tenderness and wished their own sons were a bit more like him.

VII

Uncle Frank died just before Christmas 1949. We spent that Christmas with Aunt Em at the house of another of her sisters. Aunt Em came to meet us through the hoarfroast of the bright morning. She was a lonely figure, for there were few solitary walkers that day. She took my mother's arm, while my brother and I fought for the free hand, in its glove knitted at the bedside of her dead husband. I was ten, and this was my first encounter with the need of adults for compassion. It was a disturbing moment; and she gripped our hand firmly in recognition of the small consolation we offered for her loss.

I had never been in the company of a bereaved person before. I observed her closely, not so much out of pity, as because I expected to be in a similar condition when my mother died. I wanted to know what I could learn, in order to prepare myself in advance. I could detect very little in her bearing that would help: some moments of abstraction, a weakening of her smile, a soreness around the eyes. When I thought of the bottomless grief I anticipated for myself, I concluded that her love for Uncle Frank must have been

The Uses Of Adversity

of a more measured kind; and anyway, they had only been husband and wife. It wasn't as if she had been his mother, supreme and irreplaceable. Both had been adult when they met, and I assumed that adults were not subject to the hostage-taking of the feelings of others in the way that mine had been taken from birth into my mother's custody. But Aunt Em's loss threw its pallid mantle over the festival; and although the game of Newmarket on Christmas afternoon took place as usual, the gusto with which pennies were lost or won, was muted; and when Aunt Em got the wishbone from the chicken, she gave it to my brother and me, since it was clear that the only wish she could possibly make would be impossible of fulfilment.

Uncle Frank had drawn a naval pension for the disability incurred in the course of duty, and his widow continued to draw it. In any case, he had saved and invested money; much of his inactive life had been devoted to making sure his wife would not want; and he became proficient in using the surplus from their modest requirements to ensure her years of selflessness would not be unrewarded.

Aunt Em's bereavement occurred at the same time as Sid's formal desertion – even the manner of their separation from their respective husbands contained a sharp moral lesson – it was perhaps inevitable that we would become suitable objects for her now unrequited charity. Immediately after Frank's death, I went into town every Saturday morning, to deliver one or two orders to customers who had remained loyal to my mother from the time when she had been a cook for the men in the slaughterhouse where Sid worked. I would then go to Aunt Em's house, where we had what she called 'lunch.' This was a meal, at the ceremony of which I marvelled, since she decorated the fillet of cod with a sprig of parsley and a round of tomato – culinary ornaments my mother would have scorned. She also set napkin rings at the side of our places, and placed on the table a spike of yellow winter jasmine or a Christmas rose – remnants of the small festive touches, by means of which she had celebrated with Uncle Frank his survival to share yet another day. Delicate and understated in all she did, her eyes shone when I walked in the door, and I cannot remember any such other spontaneous exhibition of pleasure at the sight of my often miserable person.

After lunch, we went to the cinema. We went, without discrimination, at the same time, every Saturday, usually entering the auditorium in the middle of the film, any film. It was the custom of people to go to 'the pictures', as though these were discrete, unconnected images in an album. In any case, plots were formulaic, and it was rarely more difficult to catch up with what had occurred than it was to anticipate was to come. It might be a murder film with Edward G. Robinson, a costume drama with Stewart Granger, a Western or even a misnamed British 'thriller', achromatic (in every sense) products, in which a woman in a fur coat walked through a deserted Mayfair at three o'clock in the morning, followed by the shadowy individual you knew was about to kill her.

After the pictures, we went on the bus to Kingsthorpe, then walked the last mile to White Hills, past the recreation ground, the 'fever hospital', when we held our breath for superstitious fear of airborne germs, and the cemetery, to the shop, where my mother would be cleaning down the mortuary-like slabs where the meat had stood, and wiping the steel rails from which the shanks of dead animals hung. The house smelt of animal fat and the spices used to smother the inferior meat in sausages. Aunt Em always brought some little treat, rock cakes or cream buns dusted with castor sugar; and she remained with us till Monday morning.

Partly as a consequence of the success of these weekends, and my mother's inability to manage the shop – she was about forty five by this time – it seemed natural that we should go to live with Aunt Em. Aunt Em, generous and gentle, opened what had been a sedate house of sickness to her sister and children. If she ever regretted it, there was never a whisper of disloyalty. Her most extreme expression of displeasure, when she wanted to conciliate our mother, in a rage about some trivial but symbolic affront, was 'Well, you know what she is.' The house had to be fumigated after Frank's death, so it posed no risk of infection; a purification ritual which, however, did not rob it of its character of shrine to my aunt's undead tenderness.

VIII

When they first lived together, my mother and her sister took pleasure in each other's company. They would play nap in the evening, a card game which involved a mild element of gambling. They talked constantly – memories of childhood, the conduct of neighbours, how much Em had paid for half a pound of butter, and where it might be had more cheaply. They kept rigorous accounts, and at the end of each day reckoned up to the last halfpenny how much they owed one another. They were to spend thirty five years together, longer than either spent with her husband. It seemed they had done the right thing and might settle into easy companionability.

It was not to last. Just as our mother had constantly corrected me and my brother, she now set about her sister, whose shortcomings cried out – to her at least – to be addressed. And she devoted herself to this with the moral rigour and practical efficiency which she had always shown. Her Puritanism required no sacred underpinning; it flowered in the secular ascesis of a deprived age.

Since Aunt Em's husband had spent his years of idle debility looking after their financial affairs, it was perhaps inevitable that his views became more conservative with time. The social consequences of this very modest shift were more far-reaching than any simple change of political colour. For Aunt Em, who made friends effortlessly, had become part of a group of women who visited each other's houses on Tuesday afternoons to play bridge and take tea together. There were delicate sandwiches and such dainty cakes as the severe mid-century afforded, and rose-patterned tea-sets like miniature funerary urns. Aunt Em had met these friends, either through her attendance at the Saxon church of St Peter's, or at the Old Guides Association, and were of a more genteel disposition than most of the women of West Street. All lived in houses much bigger than ours, close to the Park, addresses associated with superior social standing. Aunt Em was attracted by their manners – they didn't swear, and were as remote as could be from the working class in which she had been born. Ideology was, it seemed, as much a matter of temperament as conviction. Aunt Em was drawn to forms of behaviour and observances that appealed to her. When she was with her friends (my mother used the diminishing word 'pals'), she did indeed become a different person. She had an affected little laugh, and her voice (never harsh) became softer, as she imitated the vowels and patterns of speech of her companions, some of whom had been tutored, in order not to betray her origins (in one sense) in the company of their husbands' business associates, by teachers of elocution, who had thriving practices in that town of badly mauled vowels.

It was my aunt's turn to entertain once a month. On those days, my mother remained in the kitchen, washing or scouring, engaged upon some noisy domestic activity calculated to contrast with what she regarded as the wasteful pastime, the tittle-tattle, as she called it, of the women in the other room. She clattered her bucket in competition with the tinkle of teacups, innocent laughter and the bids of the card-players. The game of bridge was not serious. It gave an excuse to meet, to remember their youth and share the pity and sweetness of life.

Glad resolved to put a stop to these frivolous parties. She ob-

The Uses Of Adversity

jected on two grounds. They trivialised life, which was sombre and serious (Aunt Em knew all about that), and these women thought their arse didn't hang in the same place as everybody else's. They were, she declared, vapid and artificial. They were stuck up and they were only patronising Aunt Em, because by deigning to visit her little house in West Street, they were in a better position to relish the superiority of their own address.

They stopped coming. Aunt Em explained that now her sister and her boys were living with her, it wasn't really convenient. They understood perfectly. Little by little, her modestly joyful spirit was crushed. She became a shadow in the house in which her radiant unobtrusive presence had sustained Uncle Frank for a quarter of a century. She went about the business of emptying the pos (we had an outside lavatory) into a green enamel bucket every morning, making the beds, fetching the greens and sweeping the snow from the front pavement in winter. My mother took over the preparation of meals, and did away with the small decorative touches with which her sister had transformed these bare functional feasts into little festivals.

The house of love became a house of correction. My mother also put a stop to one of her sister's most charitable acts. When our Gran died, her son, Harry, had stayed at home; but since he was considered incapable of boiling an egg or making a cup of tea, Aunt Em had offered him a hot mid-day meal three times a week, which he ate during the break from the shoe-factory where he worked.

Harry was 'uncouth', as even Aunt Em admitted. When he and his siblings were young, there had been little time for the refinements of table manners, and Harry continued all his life to eat with noisy and messy enjoyment, spreading the remains of his oxtail stew across the table, and spitting things he did not relish onto the wooden-block floor, from which all carpets had been removed during Uncle Frank's illness, since, it was believed, these harboured germs. On days when Harry came, the table was spread with newspaper. Aunt Em thought it her duty to feel this rough and laconic churl, but my mother disagreed. 'I don't want to be slaving for him', she said, 'without a word of thanks.' Thanks, she well knew, were what men considered beneath them to offer up for the services of women, wives, mothers, sisters. Glad said he was disgusting. We children were repelled and fascinated. He had lost the top joint of his middle finger in an accident with a clicking knife, and he would use the stump for resting places for morsels of food which he then popped into his mouth; and after eating, he sprinkled snuff in the same spot and inhaled it vigorously. When his sisters deplored this habit, he would say that sneezing was his only pleasure. His fingers were stained a dark orange by nicotine, and he exuded the smell of animal hides with which he worked. It was made clear to him that he was no longer welcome. In this way, my mother established the convention that she wanted nothing to do, either with people who thought they were above her, or with people who were demonstrably below her. In fact, she didn't want much to do with anyone at all, apart from her sons and her sister, who fell under her doleful tyranny that was, she believed, purely for their own good.

IX

In spite of her vanished happiness, Aunt Em was still animated by a compassionate interest in the lives of others. Since the modest sociability she had anticipated in her home by the presence of her sister and nephews had failed to take place, she sought relief elsewhere. Because Uncle Frank had provided the means for her to live, she did so without a qualm, since she had discharged all the obligations prompted by love and duty. Although my mother had the tangible presence of her fulfilment in life, in the form of her sullen, subdued sons, Aunt Em exuded the self-confidence of those who have been happy; she wore the traces of her remembered joy like an aura. This must have galled Glad beyond endurance.

Aunt Em gained the reputation – crafted by our mother – for being flighty and gadding about. She went on pathfinding coach tours to Italy, and came back from Capri with the story that Gracie Fields had graciously descended from her villa on the cliff-top and sung 'Sally' for her admirers gathered below. She continued to go to church until, suddenly, it seemed, it became too dangerous for women to venture out alone after dark, even on so innocent an errand as an act of worship. She belonged to the Women's Institute, and came back with jars of jam, pickles and bottled fruits; activities as far as can be imagined from the dissolute and wasteful occupations my mother considered them to be.

Aunt Em also had fur coat, which she fetched out of its mothballs every November. It was tied at the waist with silk ribbons, so that no buttons disfigured the smooth fabric. It was an extravagance, no doubt, and quite inappropriate for West Street, for which gabardine and felt were considered adequate protection against the cold. My mother told her she was putting herself at risk of being robbed if she insisted on parading herself in such a get-up. It reeks of money she said. Eventually, Aunt Em set aside the offending garment and reverted to less showy wear. I found the coat after her death, with, inside, the label of the exclusive local furrier who had provided it; its silk lining was as good as new, the fur sleek and soft. By that time, of course, the wearing of fur had been disgraced for reasons other than that it made the owner look like Lady Muck.

Thanks to the providence of Uncle Frank and Glad's savings, we were able to move into the slightly bigger house in Palmerston Road; only two or three streets away, another terraced house, but to eyes practised in the subtle social distinctions of or town, a significant rise in the world. Built in the 1870s on the site of old orchards, these houses had longer gardens, and the extensions built behind as shoemakers' workshops made spacious kitchens. The lavatory was still outside, and enclosed only in the late 1960s, by which time, to go out of doors for such necessities was to occupy property unfit for human habitation.

Em's mobility only emphasized my mother's reluctance to leave the house. She suffered from something more than agoraphobia; it was a fear of not being securely within the four walls which held her entire life, even if her twins and her wandering sister perversely preferred the world outside, in Em's case, the meretricious distractions of making jam and cakes in public rather than in the privacy of her own home.

Aunt Em maintained contact with a new generation of the family, the children of cousins; a practice more generally discontinued as its members had scattered. She remembered the birthdays of great-nephews and nieces, and visited them from time to time, bearing treats and celebrating the strained bonds of kinship. She was a true conservative, in the sense that she wanted to maintain what had given her succour, the ties of blood, from which others, in a striving for liberation, were trying to escape. As it turned out, her efforts were not generally reciprocated. They probably regarded her as an old woman with little to do and time on her hands; and none of those to whom she had regularly sent small gifts at Christmas and on birthdays made an appearance at her small sad funeral.

Once a week, Aunt Em would wash my mother's hair over the kitchen sink; a towel round her shoulders, a white lather and then jugfuls of warm water to wash the soap away. At the time, there was no hot water in the house, and it had to be boiled in the kettle. One day, Aunt Em forgot to dilute the almost boiling water. The nape of my mother's neck was scalded, not seriously, since it did not blister. But she never forgave her sister, blaming the accident upon her carelessness, her distractibility, even a desire to hurt her. This became another dramatic incident in her long, slow decline. From that moment, she suffered from aggravated 'nerve trouble'. The

The Uses Of Adversity

grave opened beneath her, and she trembled upon its edge for the next thirty five years.

X

As time passed, television began to colonise their lives. The cards were put away, and brought out only when I visited with my partner, when they still enjoyed a few hands of whist. But their evenings of nap and cribbage ceased. At first, they consulted the paper to see if there was anything worth watching on TV, but later, it became their constant companion; not merely an accompaniment to their lives, but a sort of relation, bringing to them surrogate gossip, news, information and scandal which had formerly been exchanged with each other and the people of the neighbourhood who, little by little, vanished, swallowed up in personal dramas, wraiths of the social beings they had been. You could feel disintegration, not only in the community, but of the social fabric of the town itself, as the 1970s began. Security came to mean the strengthening of locks on the doors, and extra bolts and catches fastened the windows. Into the deserted spaces, where the cats howled at night and dustbin lids clattered in the wind, the dark of evening pressed with new menace against the rattling windowpanes and evil spirits hovered – muggers, rapists, burglars and addicts, which had been kept at bay as long as the streets were still populated. When the evening paper came, they turned first to the Deaths column, to see which of their acquaintances had pre-deceased them; comments on these departures were the only time when they became truly animated with each other. 'She was only 62, no age at all. I seen her in town last month and I looked at her and thought she had the shadow of the grave on her.' 'She never had much of a life did she – he knocked her about for years.' 'There was always something wrong with him, do you remember, he done time for touching them kiddies.' 'She was eighty, but she was still dinxing about town like a whore at a christening till a couple of years ago.''Of course, they were a TB family, she should never have married into them.'

Their conversations became a valedictory lament on the decayed social relationships of the provincial town. Television not only turned them away from those with whose lives their own had been entwined, but its insistent excitements, its passions and dramas appeared as an oblique comment on their own uneventful lives, lives that had, until then, circled around immediate, if less dramatic, happenings – the house-fire in the next street, the marital infidelity of a neighbour, the woman caught shoplifting, the stolen bicycle and the unknown father of a young woman's baby; pallid occurrences now they were caught up in exaltations on a grander scale – murders, obsessions, gangland robberies, epic love-stories in country-houses. TV made their own lives parochial and unsatisfying.

My mother complained more about the mild trespasses of her sister, just as she habitually lamented the shortcomings of my brother to me, and had confided my irreparable failings to him. 'I have to do all the work, she doesn't lift a finger, all she thinks about is her holidays, her life is one long holiday.' She sustained a monologue of discontent, although she herself felt insecure the minute she walked out of the front door, and was not tempted by what she saw as the shallow preoccupations of her sister, she nonetheless managed to keep up a resentment that would not be assuaged.

I was so deeply penetrated by mother's perception of the world, that I faithfully reflected her judgment of Aunt Em; and I saw through my mother's eyes her mild aspirational snobbery and posturings as her principal qualities; and I failed to appreciate her warmth and kindliness of heart, her generosity of spirit and charitable openness to the world. Later – too late – I bitterly regretted my mother's usurpation of my senses, and came to love Aunt Em more deeply. I have loved her more since her death; she taught me, posthumously, that the dead do not indeed leave us alone, and our relationship with them is far from frozen at the point when they cease to live. They continue to work on our feelings and understanding, so that nothing is finished until our own memory of them is itself effaced by death.

XI

Aunt Em lived to see herself transformed in the eyes of others, from the noble and generous woman she was into a pathetic old woman; such was the lowering of esteem in which that generation of selfless women was held by posterity. She remained with my mother until the end of her life. Glad never confided in her, never shared the secret of Sid, his shame and her own contrivances for survival. When the two old women could no longer remain in Palmerston Road, they went together into a nursing home, where they shared a room. After a few months, they complained of the claustral oppression of the building, which was a big red villa surrounded by sombre evergreens – affording a seclusion appropriate for the enjoyment of his wealth by the former boot manufacturer who built it, but less so for the elderly people, for whom it represented a seclusion from life, which they were, in any case, soon enough destined to leave.

They transferred to a purpose-built home, with picture windows overlooking a golf course, where the comings and goings of active people were constantly visible. My mother sat in her chair, elbow resting on the arm, her thumb on her right cheek, her fingers shielding here eyes from the world, a symbolic posture of withdrawal, from which she would not budge; so that the impression of the thumb on her face gave it the appearance of a patch of bright rouge. Aunt Em maintained a wan cheerfulness, as visitors became more rare, outings ceased, and friends ('so-called', as they had always been qualified by Glad). A few stragglers of our extended, but now dispersed, family, brought them the gift of their company from time to time, and the old ladies always said 'Thank you for coming' as they left, like the polite little Edwardian girls they had been.

Aunt Em became ill. There was an obstruction in her bowel. She was taken to the General Hospital, where she remained a few weeks, but there nothing but palliative care could be given to a woman of ninety. The geriatric ward to which she might have gone – in the old Workhouse which was at the top of our street – had been closed down by cuts to the health service in the 1980s, so she was sent back by ambulance to the nursing home. It was a sleety November day, and the old lady looked with weary eyes at the wet trees, their black branches covered with icy silver beads. This was to be her last view of the world. When she arrived, my mother would not have her back in the shared room. She said she would be disturbed by the presence of her sister, and so Aunt Em was placed in a separate room. She died the same night.

Born in 1899, she was cremated on a fine December day in 1989. Many of those at her sparsely attended funeral were friends of mine from childhood; few upon whom she had expended her sympathy and compassion were present. Of course, many had died; but her comforting myths with which she had perhaps consoled herself, about bread cast upon the waters, proved untrue. Her pity for, and patience with, the sufferings of others, uncelebrated in that busy, self-absorbed town, were not less significant than those of people in more exalted places, but they had to be, for this sweet, wronged woman, their own lonely reward.

PART THREE

I

While my mother served in the shop, I sat in a corner of the black and white tiled floor, reading old newspapers which people brought in for use as wrapping-paper for the meat. The estate gave a hint of the mobility that was to become more widespread after the War, since many of the papers they brought had been forwarded by relatives from the places people had left – Wales, the North East, Scotland. They had fled depression and unemployment, but at that time, they appeared almost as intruders in our settled town, with its distinctive regional voice, its sparse joys and puritanical hatred of any display, emotional as well as material; people, heavy, slow and stuck in the Midland clay out of which it seemed they had been shaped.

As I looked at the old newspapers, I learned that Wilson, Keppel and Betty were appearing at the Glasgow Empire, that Douglas Byng could be seen as Mother Goose at the Newcastle Theatre Royal, and that Charlie Cairoli was on at the Swansea Grand. I spent hours in the shop, half absorbed in regional news about knifings in Glasgow, thefts of lead from chapel roofs in South Wales, the apprehension of a bigamist in North Shields, who had left a number of grieving wives on the long string of the A6, up and down which his work as commercial traveller had taken him.

This was a rather savourless pastime; the real instruction was to be gained from listening to what passed between my mother and her customers, especially the women. As soon as I became aware of a murmured hum of sympathy from my mother, I would be all attention, although the significance of some of the whispered stories escaped me. The shop was silent, apart from the purring of the fridge, and a long susurration which, although I missed the details, was impossible not to understand as a story of the pain, loss and grief of women.

Mrs Graham was a thin, gaunt woman, whose hands constantly played with the purse she held in front of her apron. She wore her hair in a twist of scarf; her slippers were of a dingy fleece and she wore no stockings, so that a network of tiny blue veins could be seen at her ankles, like the tributaries of rivers we drew in geography lessons.

She spoke always with a suppressed, breathless urgency. If another customer appeared, she would laugh loudly, displaying large grey teeth, as though she were enjoying herself so much she could not bear to leave the place of entertainment. It appeared that she had got up one night and found her husband in the room of their only daughter, a girl of twelve. He told her he must have been sleepwalking, and didn't know where he was. She believed him; and when it happened a second time, she gave him the benefit of the doubt. But after that, she resolved to stay awake. Three nights in succession, her husband crept out of bed and went into their daughter's room.

Mrs Graham was repelled and incredulous. She insisted they had what she referred to as 'a normal married life.' She told herself that her husband was merely comforting the child who had always suffered from nightmares. But the suppressed knowledge of her husband's darker purpose was making her ill. She developed a nervous tic that convulsed one side of her mouth. Her hair began to fall out. 'Look', she would say, tearing at tufts from her scalp, 'it's coming out in handfuls'. She couldn't talk to him about it. She loved him. She loved her daughter too, of course, but she feared that if she confronted him, he would leave her. If she went to the police, there would be a court case, he would go to prison. She tried to tell herself

The Uses Of Adversity

he wasn't doing anything to the child any father might not do. He was just cuddling her.

Glad told her it was not right. It could ruin her daughter's life. 'I don't want to lose him.' 'Better lose him than see your only child's life wrecked', my mother said. She never had any doubt as to where her allegiances lay. When she was fourteen, Mrs Graham's daughter became pregnant. They said she had been attacked by a man in the woods several months before, but had never mentioned any sexual assault. There had been a story in the local paper, pictures of the stricken parents. There was talk of a fund being set up. The woman stopped coming into the shop, and the family disappeared from the neighbourhood. 'Where did they go?' I asked my mother when the next instalment of the story failed to unfold. 'High Street, China'. Then she said sharply 'You shouldn't be listening to grown up conversations.' I assured her I never heard a word, I was too busy reading the newspapers.

Beneath the surface decorum of the estate, a secret life of disorder and chaos emerged from the conversations in the shop, made manifest only in whisperings that produced little mushrooms of breath in the cold air of the shop. Tessie's husband had died in another woman's bed, a widow whose husband had been killed in the war. He had been visiting her, if that is the right word, said Tessie grimly, for several years. One day, in the widow's bedroom, he had complained of feeling tired. He closed his eyes and died in the big double bed. The widow, a thoughtful and prudent woman, had not wanted to cause pain to Tessie, whom she claimed as her best friend. Somehow, she had dressed him and dragged him downstairs, seated him upright in a chair. Tessie admired presence of mind like that at such a time. The widow was a small woman, no longer young, and Tessie's husband weighed fifteen stone. Tessie could not imagine how she had lifted him and replaced his clothing. Had the neighbours heard the rhythmic bumping of the corpse on the stairs? How had she carried him to the winged armchair, where he was found by the doctor? Even more admirably, she had prepared a cup of coffee, which she had placed, half-empty, on the table beside him. Only then had she alerted the doctor who had come immediately and sent for an ambulance. The coffee was her gesture of regret and respect to Tessie, who had to be fetched from the factory where she was working. Tessie admitted that nobody, perhaps even herself, would have doubted the innocence of this visit, since he was an electrician; but she could not but observe that in her haste, the widow had put his boots on the wrong feet.

II

These (non-business) transactions were echoed in what passed between my mother and her sisters on Thursday afternoons. For that day the shop was shut, and Aunt Em, Aunt May, Aunt Laura and sometimes Aunt Win would visit. I hurried home from school, because Aunt May – who was my mother's closest companion and counsellor in her drama with Sid – always brought something special for tea, some pieces of unidentifiable wartime confectionery made with simulated jam, artificial fat, false icing and imitation cream; the war, a period of such inescapable reality, was also a time of the counterfeit of almost everything. These unappetising treats were not the real pleasure of the afternoon, which lay in listening to what passed between the whispering giantesses above me. I was supposed to be playing with plasticine, and I kept my eyes firmly on the pattern of the carpet, its brown-and-orange zigzags. In the presence of adult conversations, children were assumed to be shielded by their innocence from all understanding. I acquired a functional absence, which meant giving the impression of such preoccupation that they would sometimes break off and say reassuringly 'Look, he lives in a world of his own.' If I did, it was a world composed entirely of images, allu-

The Uses Of Adversity

sions and suggestions they made; and it was far from the comforting place which they imagined I inhabited.

As they spoke, whole networks of relationships sprang into existence. The conjured ramifying genealogies out of a funeral that had taken place the week before; evoked the rise and extinction of whole families from a piece of gossip heard in the town centre. Between them, they knew everyone in Northampton; and this was no sketchy knowledge-system in a population of ninety thousand. They were aware of the state of everyone's health, most people's marriage and a great many individuals' financial situation. A considerable exchange of information took place. The biographies of individuals were amended and added to, according to the most recent data; whole lives re-assembled out of speculation and projection. There was something wonderfully creative in the zest with which they passed in review the fate of others.

Their conversations were dramatic and theatrical; at times they spoke with a choral elliptical gravity; stylised performances; their own ritual versions of poetry and art. I can hear them now, more than sixty years later, morbid and sepulchral, with glimpses of macabre humour.

Much of their conversation was about deaths and the secrets of parentage revealed by pieces of paper that fluttered down from behind a clock when an old woman's house was sold; revelations about illegitimacies, half-brothers and half-sisters, stepfathers whose existence rendered wills invalid, made paupers out of those who had confidently expected to come into a fortune, and visited riches on those resigned to a lifetime of poverty. They often dwelt on their own extinction; sober consideration of the brevity of human life stood them in the stead of blighted religious beliefs, and had to serve as an austere consolation for an eternity of which they had been robbed by the secular convictions with which their own experience had burdened them.

III

One Wednesday afternoon, her sister May came into the shop. Glad was annoyed. Didn't she know Wednesday was one of the busiest days of the week. That particular week – it was June 1938 – May had already come on Monday. Although she lived on the same estate, barely ten minutes walk away, she would never appear like this without good reason. Their visits followed their own rhythm, and a call outside of the expected regular acknowledgements of intimacy meant hat something dramatic had happened. May had appeared restless and agitated; on the verge of saying something. Glad had not encouraged her to speak. Sensing her sister's hostility, May had gone away without unburdening herself. My mother saw her on the Wednesday afternoon through the shop window, wearing a felt hat and a pinafore over her skirt. It was the custom of the time for women to wear a hat indoors, as though permanently expecting to be called away urgently, although they rarely went anywhere.

Aunt May was like my mother, strong-willed, dominating, self-righteous, but at the same time, honest, incorruptible and 'straight', as they self-flatteringly called themselves. As a child, I was terrified of upsetting my mother, who let it be known that her love for us, indeed, her life itself, depended upon our complete obedience to everything she demanded of us. She tolerated no waywardness and no contradiction. I never dared put to the test the possible connection between any misbehaviour I might contemplate and my mother's survival; and I never vexed or opposed her in any way. But such docility could not exist without its opposite. Accordingly, whenever I was left with Aunt May, I would sometimes challenge or defy her. She served as a proxy for my mother. Sometimes, I would 'show off', a general term which indicated the behaviour of any child who drew attention to itself. This was as close as I could

The Uses Of Adversity

come with impunity to breaking the absolute taboo on upsetting my mother.

Aunt May would sometimes look at me with a troubled frown which clearly let me know she thought I had been excessively indulged and needed a damn good hiding. There was little physical resemblance between the sisters; but they shared the same moral character, an invincible sense of their own rectitude; a likeness in character so striking that people often mistook one for the other. On one of her last excursions to town, my mother had been in Boot's, and a woman approached her, calling her by her sister's name. 'No, I'm Gladys. May died ten years ago.' The stranger then explained that she was psychic, and that May had a message for her. My mother, affronted by the idea that if her sister wanted to communicate with her, dead or not, she would not select this impudent stranger as her messenger. She said coldly 'What's that then?' The woman said 'She tells you that she'll never be dead as long as you're alive.'

May was possessed of something she cold no longer keep to herself, however strongly her sister resisted hearing it. Glad protested that she had her hands full. There was a shop full of meat waiting to be cut up, according to the 10 pence ration, to which each registered customer had been reduced in the hardships of the post-war world. And then the delivery note had not corresponded to what she had actually received. The men who brought the meat from the wholesalers were taking some of the best cuts, imagining that she, a woman on her own, would not notice ---

May was insistent, cutting through her sister's objections. 'His lorry has been parked in the same place, five nights in a row.' Glad shrugged and said 'His lorry has been parked outside half the houses in the county.' 'Not outside this one.'

Glad had, earlier in the week, rejected May's efforts to tell her what she knew; an unusual act of repudiation because they thrived on a kind of unofficial under-knowledge of the life of the neighbourhood. The women of the estate were always particularly quick on the trail of any irregular sexual conduct. It was their duty (they said) to report anything they heard, or saw, or thought they herd or saw, or that anyone else heard or saw, to the injured party; an undertaking they carried out with ceremonial relish. Glad thought May must be the carrier of tidings that Sid had become less prudent in his wanderings, and had perhaps sought consolation closer to home than previously. But the tone of May's voice compelled her to ask, sharply 'Where was that then?' 'It was outside the doctor's.' Glad said it was a pity her sister had nothing better to do than keep count of where he parked his truck. 'There must be something wrong with him.' Glad suggested this was not news to her; but she spoke only to delay the disclosure, to prepare a response behind which she could hide her reaction. She found herself trembling with apprehension. 'He's sick, duck. Why else would he be at the doctor's every evening?' 'What is it then?' 'How should I know?' 'You seem to know everything else.' 'That's up to you to find out.' 'May my duck, I'm past caring.' 'You shouldn't be. It might affect you.' 'What?' 'He might have caught something. Something dangerous.'

May had spoken what her sister already knew; and this made her angry. She had once become aware of a terrible itch in the groin, and discovered he had given her crab-lice. She had washed herself in water as hot as she could bear. It scalded her flesh but did not remove the lice. Someone (a customer in the shop?) had told her that alcohol would kill them. She bought half a bottle of whisky, and drenched herself in it. It worked. When she confronted Sid, he was all innocence, and even accused her of going with another man. 'When would I have a chance to do that?' she cried. Sid was adept at denying the obvious, and could not bear to acknowledge himself culpable in anything. He found it difficult to accept the consequences of his own actions, making elaborate excuses which left everyone wondering at his infantile efforts at evasion. Glad said to

The Uses Of Adversity

May 'Well it doesn't affect me.' 'Does that mean you don't have anything to do with him, *that way*?' 'You mind your business.' 'It is my business.'

It was, too. My mother's sisters had a keen sense of duty to one another, and they walked in and out of each other's lives as they went in and out of one another's houses, without knocking, without announcing themselves. It seemed, sometimes, that their lives were common land; and it was up to them to keep it well cultivated, free from pests or neglect. What would now be considered unwarrantable interference in other people's conduct was simply an aspect of family commitment. If one was believed even to be contemplating any departure from the path of marital virtue, her sisters saw themselves as justified in warning her to desist, in ordering the potential adulterer to bugger off, even in telling a tyrannical husband. This led to some fierce arguments and bitter quarrels; but the storms soon blew over, for the feeling that each existed to keep the others from harm was always stronger.

May said wisely 'You can catch it off cups. The lavatory. I know. I know a woman who got it, and she had never been with a man.' 'Well, if you're that interested, why don't you ask him?' 'All right', said May, 'I will.' 'Don't you bloody dare.'

May, having performed an unpleasant duty, not without the grim righteousness of those untainted by the tales they have to bear, went away. Glad had had her suspicions that something was wrong. That past week, Sid had come home every evening, and had not gone out again. Normally, he would stay in the house only an hour or two, shave with the cut-throat razor he sharpened on a leather strap, lather his face and wipe the grey-coloured scrapings onto a piece of toilet paper, and then be off again, saying 'Don't wait up.' His recent attachment to the home suggested something was seriously amiss.

IV

When he came home, she laid the table and set his meal before him. Rabbit stew. Sid was an accomplished poacher. He kept a ferret, and excursions from which he returned with a sack full of wriggling rabbits helped augment the meagre meat ration; the skins could also be sold to the rag and bone man for threepence each, which Sid used for drinking-money. Glad sat down at the opposite side of the table, her face flushed with embarrassment. She hoped for some excuse, some explanation. When none came, she asked why he had been to the doctor's so often.

Angrily, he got up, knocked the chair over and asked why she had been spying on him. Her eyes, he said, were never off him. They were everywhere. He couldn't even sit down in the evening without feeling her stare burning into him. What was the matter with her? Why wouldn't she let him be?'

She said 'Finish your dinner.' He sat down. 'Tell me what's wrong Sid.'

Now he became tearful. She had never seen him cry. He hadn't wanted to tell her, because he was afraid it would worry her. He had been to the doctor because of an infection that would not clear up. He thought he had caught it from rabbits. The doctor had advised him not to go rabbiting for a while, although catching rabbits, he said virtuously, was one of the few enjoyments he still had in life. There was a rash on his body. Some sores. It would soon clear up. You have to be careful with wild animals, he said.

My mother had been so eager to hear good news that relief submerged every other feeling. May, that prophet of doom, had never liked Sid. Who could tell what her motive was in bringing these warnings to her? She should have enough to think about with her own husband, who was out all hours, playing darts and drinking; he wasn't exactly in a hurry to get home in the evening either.

The Uses Of Adversity

That was because that bloody witch offered him little incentive to do so. She would have a go at her next time she saw her on her own. Glad felt elated. She had worried about nothing.

Sid didn't go out that evening either. She prepared for bed. He had moved into the spare room, because, he said, considerately, he arrived home at all hours, and didn't want to disturb her when she had to get up so early in the morning. Glad lay still in the big double bed. That was like a catafalque, a sacrificial altar. She waited to see what he would do. She heard him come upstairs. He knocked at the door, and she smiled at the quaint decorousness of his respect. It had been a long time since they had slept together. It felt almost like a homecoming. He came in, but was in no hurry to get into bed. She looked at his face. There were creases at the corner of the eyes, a greater fullness in the familiar contours, and the hairline had begun to rise on his forehead. He sat down on the bedcover and took her hand.

She shivered. Sid had been moved by her readiness to believe him, and knew that he, well practised in deceit, would never be able to sustain the lie he had told her. He began to talk. 'Glad. It's something else.' 'What?' 'It wasn't rabbits.' She understood at once, as indeed, of course she had known even while she was covering her knowledge with the short-lived gaiety she had permitted herself in response to his excuses. She said harshly 'No, I never thought for a minute it was.' She waited. A heavy silence fell between them, an impermeable tension that would never again be lifted. 'Well?' 'I got it from…a woman.' 'What is it?' 'The doctor says', he began as though the doctor were at fault', 'it's sexually transmitted.' 'Oh.' 'Yes. He says it's something called' – he pretended to search for a word that was unknown to him – 'syphilis'. 'Oh no.' She threw back the bedclothes, and trembling, threw a dressing-gown around her shoulders. 'I think we'd better go downstairs.'

She knew then that the rupture in their relationship, sexual and emotional, would never be mended. A feeling of utter desolation swept over her; but it was tinged with curiosity about what had happened to him. She had never thought of herself in relation to any other man. Later, she would become resentful. Women go and commit themselves to one man, the wrong man, always the wrong man; and then, when it proves disastrous – and when doesn't it? – we are left stranded, our feelings stuck to them like flies on sticky paper.

She made a quick calculation. There had been no sexual contact between them for well over a year. The wave of desire that had shaken her an hour earlier had spent itself. His teeth shone in the darkness. His eyes were clear, his dark hair glistened, iridescent in the electric light. She contrasted what she had just heard with the way he looked; more beautiful than ever. He would never touch her again.

He had been ill for two years, but had denied it. During that time, his life of erotic nomadism had been uninterrupted as he travelled across the country in his lorry. He had some names and addresses of women, all over the Midlands, some as far away as Yorkshire, scrawled on pieces of paper, even scratched into the dashboard of the truck, accompanied by a heart pierced with an arrow. Many were false. Others proved untraceable. The hospital almoner later tried to compile a list of all those he could remember. There were seventeen, eighteen; many he couldn't recall. The almoner had undertaken to write to them, informing them of the risk they ran, advising them to have an urgent health check.

Syphilis had already passed into its tertiary stage. There was tissue loss to the roof of the mouth and the mucous membranes. He would have to undergo a course of injections, for an indefinite period, a compound of arsenic and mercury. That would ultimately halt the damage, although the destroyed soft tissue would never be restored. The infection would clear, but it would not do so quickly. He would be required to attend hospital three or four times a week. He would have to give up work, at least in the early months of treatment. He must on no account have sexual relations with any-one. He was frightened, as much as by the prohibition on what had become an addiction (would he be able to abstain?), as by the in-definite future of painful injections. He wept. Glad, what am I go-ing to do?

She was overwhelmed by anger and an obscure culpability. How little she had been able to do to help him, driven as he was, by this strange (male?) impulse to go from town to town, from woman to woman, in search of something which, she still felt, she ought to have been able to provide for him. What was wrong with her, that she had been unable to still this compulsion in him? She experi-enced a new sense of inadequacy – was she so unattractive, was she repulsive to him? It must be her fault that he had embarked on this reckless spending spree of desire. She always felt that his attraction to her must have been based upon a mistake, some misapprehen-sion. Now, it seemed, she had been revealed in her true colours; and they were drab and repelling. The pitiful pride she had taken in being able to draw someone like him to her, how vain and boastful it now seemed. She despised her own efforts to understand, through novels and poetry, how human attractions arise and fade away, her pitiful belief that any of that would be of assistance to her in living!

She said nothing of this to him, since he would only too grate-fully have accepted her self-accusation, and would have found relief and justification if she had admitted her own inability to control his incontinence. She felt there were limits to the degree of humiliation to which she would let him see her descend; a restraint which later, helped her to reconstruct her life, although in ways which, at that moment of revelation, which was like a daybreak over some scene of nocturnal storms, she could not possibly have foreseen.

She, too, was summoned to the hospital for tests. After an un-bearably tense and fretful two weeks, she was told there was no trace of infection in her. She was grateful to have been unpolluted by the malady that must have affected many of the women who had, no doubt, welcomed his story, whatever it was, of being alone, unattached, a wanderer on the face of the earth, and offered him solace for his outcast state. She thought grimly of their husbands and boy-friends, and imagined another network of kinship, people related to one another by poisoned blood. She tried to resist the moral advantage her own immunity gave her; since this did little to address the problem of how she was to lead the rest of her life.

During those two weeks of waiting, she pondered her limited choices. She apologised to May, who wept and comforted her. From that time, until her death from leukaemia in 1964, May was to be her only confidante, the only repository of a secret which would remain with her, until she told my brother and me some thirty five years later; by which time, it had become compounded by other necessary, and increasingly contorted, concealments. For a few weeks, she went numbly about her work. It seemed at first her situation was without remedy. But within a short space of time, encouraged by her sister, and the will not to submit passively to fate, she found reservoirs of energy within herself to devise a strategy, which would require much planning and forethought if it were to be carried out successfully.

V

She was already thirty four. Her first fear was that she would never now have children. There had been two miscarriages within three years. She had not conceived again, and in any case, their sexual relationship had already begun to wane. She wondered if the miscarriages had turned him against her. It had been sudden and unexpected, and she barely had time to realise she was pregnant. She had wakened one cold February morning with severe pains. She

The Uses Of Adversity

was in the shop, but felt weak, and went to make herself some hot milk. She was on the sofa when the haemorrhage occurred. Sid was serving. He came in and in his panic, fetched some newspapers they used for wrapping meat. Then he called the doctor. He had looked at her then, she recalled, as though from an immense distance; not the distance that always exists between men and women, that gulf out of which is generated the perpetual renewal of desire; but she had felt something else in his regard: contempt for a woman who could not even carry his babies.

She thought at first she might wait until Sid recovered, but shuddered at the idea. Not only was this an unlikely expectation – it could be years before he was well enough for sexual relations – but she herself was now revolted by him. The good looks and slender body only mocked the inner decay, as she saw it. She identified him with the sickness that was, literally, devouring him from within; a kind of culpable consumption, a self-inflicted version of what had stricken Frank.

He stayed at home. He lay on the sofa, toying with the role of invalid. She would have none of it. This was an illness to be punished rather than nursed, and she set about it with vengeful zeal. He didn't know what to do with himself. She felt herself weaken with pity: his utter resourcelessness gave her, she thought, some insight into the promiscuity of his relationships. Sex was the only thing he was good at; not even that; merely being attractive, and that he could certainly claim no credit for. That was a gift (was it?) of God or nature. He opened a book and read the first page or two of some Westerns by Zane Grey. He looked at the horse-racing column in the Daily Express. He stood by the window and watched the rain, like a child whose parents had forbidden him to go out to play.

The truth was he didn't trust himself to go out. He was possessed by his own sexual needs. He stayed close to his wife, relying on her to exercise a vigilance and control over him which he was incapable of. He sensed, with resentful admiration, her strength and endurance, and placed himself in her custody; and felt like a criminal who had surrendered. Infantilised and dependent, he chafed at his own elective captivity. It was now his turn to look at – and to – her, although with a very different watchfulness from that she had once turned on him. He was expectant, waiting to be told what to do. In a way, she learned to mother him; and my brother and I later received the same remorseless care. One day, Sid even asked her, pathetically, to read to him. She told him that if he wanted fairy-tales for grown-ups, he had better look elsewhere.

The lorry stood, unused, on blocks beside the shop. Oil spilled in rainbow splashes onto the gravel. Little pools of ochre rust formed beneath the mudguards. It remained, reproachful, symbol of his vagrant desire, vehicle of his nemesis. He covered it with tarpaulin, and the rain made a pool in the sagging material.

He decided to clear the garden. The roses had been neglected since they were first planted, when they had come to the newly built house and shop seven years earlier. Shoots and suckers that should have been pruned spread in wide thorny arcs; the flowers had become thin and papery, ghosts of the rich cream inflorescences they had been. Whenever she went to the dustbin to empty the ashes from the grate, red spikes hooked her clothes or sprang back against her hand leaving a dotted line of tiny blood-clots on the flesh.

Sid tore up everything that grew and raked the bare earth. She watched him from the window, tugging violently at cow-parsley and tenacious ground-elder that had smothered the area which was to have been lawn. The sweat silvered his face and drenched his shirt. In his labour there was a work of ineffectual atonement. She was not displeased. But now, in a reversal of their previous relationship, it was his presence that became irksome to her.

The Uses Of Adversity

VI

He began a life apart. She was able to set her own terms. She would look after him until he was fully recovered and capable of resuming work. After that, she made no promises. At the same time, she expected to be free do with her life as she pleased. This condition was accepted without protest. He had no idea of her intention; she had not even fully formed it herself. He was grateful. It was, he acknowledged, more than he had any right to expect. He said to her 'You're a good woman.' She said 'What do you know about the goodness of women? You'll see how good I am by what I do. Judge me then.'

She behaved dutifully towards him, and outwardly, nothing seemed to have disrupted their marriage. She emptied the zinc pail that stood perpetually beside the sofa, into which he coughed the mucus and slime that came from his damaged mouth. She said later that the smell of this stayed in her nostrils and would do so until the day she died. She washed it down the outside drain with half a bottle of disinfectant, so the house began to smell like a hospital ward. For him she set aside a separate plate, knife, fork and spoon, and tied cotton, a bright warning red, around the handles, so that no one else should use them. She would not go into his bedroom, and left him to wash his own sheets, which he did reluctantly and as infrequently as she allowed it. The room became rancid and feral. The rain came in at one corner of the ceiling and mildew spread its bluish blossoms on the pale patterned wallpaper.

At first, Sid could not believe his good fortune. He admitted to himself he had underestimated her. Occasionally he would be disturbed by a new resoluteness – the way she worked in the shop, the efficiency with which she cooked bland but nourishing food, kept the house clean, pursued her weekly cycle of penance; while he did nothing but monitor the progress of the sickness within, listening, waiting to assess the limit of the harm it had done, and discover how soon he could return to the wayfaring sexuality which illness had disrupted..

She seemed to have made a decision, but if she had, she did not communicate it to him. She demanded nothing of him, not even help in the twelve- or fourteen-hour days she worked. The leisure of his life was tedious to him, clouded perhaps also by the feeling that she had made some accommodation with the situation without reference to him. She certainly did not consult him or his wishes on anything. But apart from this mild discomfort, his life was easier than it had ever been. He had entrusted his weak will to her, a sickly child, and she was happy to nurse it for him.

The vacant hours which would normally have been filled with plans for sexual adventuring, remained without occupation. He was thankful for her constant presence, since it relieved him of temptation, but at times he sulked or raged, blaming her for her superintendence of his life. 'Nobody insisted that you stay Sid. You're free to leave whenever you like.' The prospect of this formless unlimited freedom filled him with dread.

She also had her secret terrors. She feared above all that one of her customers might discover the truth of Sid's illness. Even worse, she was afraid he might threaten disclosure, and with it, the ruin of the business, if she vexed him too much. She resolved not to provoke him. She need not have worried. It probably never occurred to him to do anything to disturb the unquiet calm into which their lives had settled. He was not malicious or vengeful; less so than she was; but then, he had no reason to be.

To those who asked about her husband's indisposition, she told them he had ruptured himself while unloading the lorry, and expected to be at home for some time. Three times a week he kept his hospital appointment. He sat for punitively wearying hours in an outhouse in a corner of the hospital grounds, a bare distempered room, along with other sexual miscreants, waiting for the injection

The Uses Of Adversity

of poison into his veins. He had been ordered not to drink alcohol, a privation which helped him to observe the even more strict prohibition on sexual activity.

In the time of enforced leisure, he became more reflective than he had ever been. He turned his drifting attention idly towards social and political issues which it was becoming difficult to ignore. He had until that time regarded such things as no concern of his. But he started listening to other radio programmes than racing commentaries and football scores. He asked Glad's opinion. Did she think the unemployed really didn't want to work? She said if anyone knew, he should. One day he expressed an admiration for Hitler, and was astonished by the vehemence of her opposition. Why are you getting all worked up over such thing? He asked, 'it seems all right to me. You've got to hand it to him, he's put his country on the map.

In the evenings, when the shop was closed, she came into the living room and sat in the chair by the fire. They were forced into tense conviviality; at times, even a fragile sense of security, a familiarity that was almost comforting. Sid seemed to find a voice as a result of his compulsory physical continence, and began to confide in her. As he did so, she was able to piece together what had happened.

VII

He had met a woman in a pub in town, 'a blonde with a navy-blue parting', as Glad called her. She was almost ten years older than Sid, a widow. She was, he said, lonely, having recently buried her husband. 'Where', asked Glad, 'in the back yard?' She invited Sid to the little house where she lived with her daughter, who was not quite sixteen.

Whenever Sid visited, the daughter was always present. He noticed that her mother never sent the girl out of the room. It was almost as if the young woman's presence was deliberately arranged. She didn't efface herself or sit quietly in the corner. She would flick through a magazine, do her nails, occasionally focussing upon something outside the window, so that the sun, reflected on the red brick of the houses behind, gilded her face and her distant blue eyes. The mother kept her close for reasons that did not immediately appear. Was she saying See, this is how I used to be, or was she suggesting the daughter was also available? Or was the daughter chaperone to her mother, deterring, drawing on or diverting potential lovers? Sid was intrigued, and happy to maintain his regular visits.

It was only later that the mother seemed to pay attention to her daughter, by which time it was too late. He had already infected the daughter with the gonorrhoea he had taken from her mother. When the relationship had been made transparent in this way, the mother threatened to expose him for having had sexual intercourse with a girl of sixteen. The woman insisted that the disease had nothing to do with it, but offered, as it were, only additional proof to Sid's seduction of an innocent young girl.

Even Sid was appalled by this apparent depravity. Had the mother knowingly transmitted a disease, and then allowed it to be passed on to her own daughter, just to get money from him? He was truly shocked. Somewhere, he had retained an element of country innocence; and although capable of concealment and denial, such deviousness was beyond him; this must obviously be a product of urban morality. He gave the women all the money he could lay hands on, a few hundred pounds. Glad had noticed a falling off in the weekly income, and had worked harder to bring back the money to the level from which it had declined. She listened to his story; and checked the anger that rose in her, when she realised she had been making good the money her husband had paid out in

The Uses Of Adversity

blackmail.

To his relief, the two women left town; to try, Sid imagined, their game elsewhere. He heard they had gone to Birmingham, a city which must have provided more ample scope than the limited prospects of our town. Sid had been to the hospital, and the infection was treated with sulphapyridine, known then as 'M & B tablets'. It had cleared.

As for syphilis, he did not know where he could have contracted it. There was a lesion which would not heal. He thought it was from handling wild rabbits. That had disappeared with time. He had also, for good measure, taken some patent medicines which claimed to cure sexual diseases, and when the sore vanished, he assumed the commercial remedies had done the trick. He didn't think too much about it. At the time, he had felt angry with his wife: if she had been more responsive, if she had enjoyed his body, *if she had given him what he wanted,* none of this would have happened. He blamed her for her inability to rescue him from his own devouring sexual need; and she blamed herself for being unable to rescue him, for the power to do so, she had imagined, was what love bestows upon those who love enough.

She did, however, have the ability to make Sid feel shame. Why should she? He thought he despised her, but beneath this, he felt a profound respect – for her competence, her intelligence, her ambition, everything he lacked. He resented her continence, which presented him with such opposition to his own greedy indiscipline. It made her unreachable. She knew him better than he would ever know her, but that, he told himself, was because he was open, while she hid herself, mistress of dissimulation. He felt known by her, vulnerable and uncomfortable. Occasionally he had hit her, a backhander that left a crimson flower on her cheek. Once he had splashed a cup of tea in her face, an ochre-coloured blanket that spread through the air and broke on her skin. She did not even flinch. He had never seen her cry. He vowed he would make her weep tears of self-pity, humiliation, fear. He felt a woman whose tears remained unseen was superior, particularly since he had several times broken down before her. One day, when he made to strike her, she did fall. She stayed on the ground where she lay, pretending to be more hurt than she was. Sid panicked and locked the back door. By that time, my brother and I were about seven. We had been playing in the garden, but, drawn by the noise and the sound of the key in the lock, we shaded our eyes against the window-pane and saw her horizontal, unmoving on the carpet. Sid was splashing water over what we feared was her lifeless face. At our howling, she opened her eyes, got up and opened the door; and she comforted us against the blow she had received.

When Sid had told her everything, she sat in a position of outward repose. She didn't express outrage at his conduct. She appeared unperturbed, as if they had been talking about somebody else, a piece of gossip from the shop.

Afterwards, he became apprehensive at the quietness of her resolve. What, he wondered, would she do? He thought she might be planning some terrible revenge. Would she kill him? He imagined the cold rage that would prompt her to seize a butcher's knife, one of the cleavers hanging from the steel rails in the shop. Would he wake up one night and see the blade in the moonlight as it cut the darkness before the mutilation, the pain, the emptiness? He thought she might poison him. Yes, that would be her way; no physical violence. And sure enough, one day, the dinner tasted strange. Bitter. 'What have you put in this stew?' 'What?' 'It tastes funny. What's in it?' 'Carrots, onions, potatoes, the usual.' She tried another mouthful. 'Yes, you're right.' She went into the kitchen. He had left some daffodil bulbs on the table which he had taken up from the garden, and she had absently peeled them and unthinkingly added them to the saucepan on the stove. He said 'I thought you wanted to poison me.' She replied 'There's only one poisoner in this house.' He crept away to the heap of dingy army blankets in

The Uses Of Adversity

his mildewed room, and fled into sleep, which became his refuge. He rose late and went to bed early. He had, it turned out, a gift for sleep, twelve, fourteen hours, a symmetrical time-span of her working hours. She would be still washing and scouring when he went to bed, and at the chopping block when he got up. He would say to her guiltily, gruffly 'Been at it all night have you?'

VIII

When they were young, it would have been incomprehensible to my mother and aunt that the elderly might become a major source of employment; in part, of course, because far fewer people lived to a great age. She and her sister were bewildered by the succession of Maries, Angelas and Samanthas who visited the house to put them to bed, many of whom they never saw twice. They lived to see cohorts of professionals summoned to labour in the management of old age – wardens of sheltered homes, home helps, geriatricians, researchers into 'the ageing process', as well as the chasers of the 'grey pound', the seekers after eternal youth, the makers of preparations to banish wrinkles and prolong life, builders of discreet retirement facilities in enclosures called The Pyghtle of The Retreat, providers of private pensions and holidays for the elderly, which would permit them, to sit in rainswept glass shelters in resorts bypassed by time in the middle of October.

My mother expressed her resentment as a – by then – archaic socialist convictions that her infirmity had become someone else's business opportunity. Nursing homes appeared to be the coming thing, and hotel chains and property companies were said to be investing in last-but-one resting places for the old, just as they had previously invested in shopping malls or fast-food outlets. My mother saw the old offered prospects for the rapid recycling of their life savings to a new generation of entrepreneurs, although the workers they employed were unpaid and often inexperienced. Their absence of skills reflected an increasingly neglectful attitude towards those once referred to as 'having borne the heat and burthen of the day', but now described as 'senior citizens'. 'Stick a frilly cap on their head and a badge on their jumper and call them carers', she said scornfully. 'Who's going to care for anything at £3 an hour?'

Sometimes Glad would sit in the public lounge. It was impossible to be unaware of the function of those tight circles of high-backed chairs of easily washable material, the Zimmer frames, the underlying odour of urine and disinfectant, television playing Australian soap-operas while heads fell forward on wasted chests and hands continued to work away, as though still at the bench or lathe they had left twenty years earlier. For in their fate is our future: the effect upon us of their immobility, confusion and helplessness is to make us realise how short the time is, and how we must hurry, hurry, to live life to the full, the brief years that stand between us and the catatonic stillness of the afternoon hours, when the summer breeze inhabits the net curtains and the geraniums blaze in their hanging-baskets, and the old sleep their shallow after-dinner sleep. Their purpose is to goad us to even more heroic feats of enjoyment and an appreciation of the fullness of life than we have yet known. Our very pity for them, the scantiness of their needs, propels us into a resolve to fill the hours that remain with yet more of the pleasures that alone can distract us from the certain destiny that this dereliction will one day be ours.

Most people in the home were far from having been abandoned by their families. They did not lack visitors, who brought little treats – a raspberry trifle in its little plastic goblet, a nip of whisky, a canister of lavender talcum powder. They saw awkwardly on the hard chairs beneath the chandelier of plastic candles, not quite knowing what to say next to their quarantined loved ones.

The Uses Of Adversity

Once you have asked what they had for dinner and said how nice their hair looks, and found out if they need any more Steradent or incontinence pads, there is little to say about the present; and you hesitate to start them off about the past, because if you do, there'll be no stopping them. And then, our own lives are so crowded – dinner to prepare, the car taken in for servicing, dancing class and football for the children, and your favourite programme is on at seven thirty. So you promise the grandchildren will come on Saturday, with the new school photo, the youngest looks really cheeky, you can tell he's going to be a heartbreaker....

As you step out of the Victorian house with its spacious hall and oriel windows, past the new annexe built on the site of the old coach-house, where the dark spruce-tree brushes the clear afternoon sky, it is a relief to be out in the warm sunshine. There is a new buoyancy in your step; and the desire to live while you still have your health and faculties surges through you with a powerful physical force.

IX

'You needn't come every week' my mother and aunt used to say. 'You've got your own life to lead... You can't be running up here every five minutes. We're all right.' Your own life to lead – they offered a sanctioned disengagement, as though my sweet aunt and sad mother were not part, and the most significant, of that life. How did it become so difficult to look after those we love simply because they are old? Is it because families are such depleted places, or because people are separated by the needs of work or simply a desire to be elsewhere? Are there fewer self-sacrificing single women who fulfilled such roles in the past? And were these not often assisted by a more ample circle of kin and neighbourhood, which offered them relief from constant vigil over elders? When this duty falls to a single person – and there are five million of them in Britain, mostly women – she or he becomes isolated, and caring becomes an intolerably lonely experience. My cousin, who nursed her mother till she died at ninety three, said she never slept soundly for a single night in the last twenty years of the old woman's life. She was always alert, listening, anticipating, imagining a call in the night, her sleep haunted by the image of her mother paralysed by a stroke, crying out in voiceless terror. At the end, exhausted, already old, she said 'It was a privilege to do it, I don't regret a minute of it.'

Perhaps the most convincing reason for these involuntary desertions is economic necessity; the obligation to earn a living. I could have pleaded work to justify ignoring my mother's early entreaties not to put her into a home; but what labour could be more vital than the cherishing of my mother and aunt, to whom I was bound with a profound, sorrowing helplessness? There is no answer; except that it would have been unbearable to have spent the days preparing meals, feeding them, getting them onto the commode, holding the drink that shaking hands could no longer convey to the mouth, and then listening to the changing rhythms of the breath in their disturbed sleep. But the question is still there, insistent, perhaps unanswerable - how has it come about that the most natural course of duty in the world has become to us an unbearable sacrifice, even the thought of it a torment?

The people in the nursing home were expected to be good, docile and grateful, whether or not their care was subsidised or they paid the full market rate for what they received. They were described by staff as 'naughty girls' or 'bad boys', if they failed to conform to a stereotype of resignation and humility; their obedience was preferable if it were at the same time insentient. My mother resented being infantilised. She said it is because the staff, who are young and vigorous, have to distance themselves from the residents; they want to believe this will never happen to them, and they

The Uses Of Adversity

are in a category permanently exempt from the corrosion of time.

She became, as was expected of her, self-effacing, saying she had lived to long and excusing herself for not having died sooner. Her feelings of helplessness, my sense of guilt and shame, the competence of the professionals merged in a collusive assumption that this is indeed the best of all possible worlds, although, in some secret unacknowledged place in our heart, we know better. We preferred to maintain the pretence that these were personal visitations, and our feeling of guilt remained a private worry, because this pain, keen though it was, was more tolerable than the thought that it was a consequence of social and economic developments that we, as individuals, could no more control than we could command the waves.

Jeremy Seabrook

PART FOUR

I

One sunshiny morning in early summer, she stood at the kitchen window, which stood open to the field at the side of the shop. It was brilliant with buttercups and the pale moth-like flowers of the blackberry briars. Glad looked up from her washing and saw a man at the window. He had a full, rather fleshy face, with a moustache and receding fair hair. He was smiling. Startled, she recoiled and splashed some greasy water onto her apron. He apologised for disturbing her, but could he trouble her for a bucket of water? Instead of coming to the door to hand her the pail, he lifted it through the window. His eyes were dark blue. He was, he told her, working on the nearby building site. The tap had run dry and water was needed for cement.

He returned several times during that morning. He was involved in the construction of a new roadhouse, about two hundred yards up the road. He had actually designed the building, but said that he didn't believe in asking other people to do any work he could not do himself. He had begun his working life as a labourer, and still enjoyed the exhilaration of manual effort, the feeling of exhausted satisfaction it yielded. The new building was, he said, to be a completely new idea of a drinking place, nothing like the traditional pub, gateway to instant, joyless escape with its frosted glass and sawdust. There would be a winter garden, with palm trees and evergreens in tubs. It would boast a lounge and, exotic harbinger of

119

things to come, a car park; in keeping with the new and more ample life anticipated for the future. He expounded his views with an enthusiasm which thrilled her. We were about to enter a more sophisticated age, where working people would begin to demand things, small luxuries previously reserved for the rich. What had been seen as too good for the common people would become the staples of daily life. He spoke with a quiet passion, which few men had ever considered her worthy of; and if she thought such uplifting sentiments misplaced in what was, after all, a structure intended for the consumption of alcohol, she forbore to mention it.

Impressed by his energy, the vague plans she had been formulating in her mind suddenly took material shape. She became animated. His interest in her was obvious. The trouble he had taken to explain his vision, the smile as his eyes sought hers, suggested at once that this might be no casual encounter. Their conversation was interrupted by each pail of water he fetched, and then resumed where it had left off. She lingered in the kitchen, although there was work to be done in the shop. As he collected his third or fourth bucket of water, she said 'Isn't your idealism a bit misplaced? It's still a pub.' 'No, no. This is relaxation for the ordinary man. Why should it be without dignity or comfort'? 'But drink.' She grimaced, and said all the men in her family had been too partial to milk from the brown cow, and this had denied their families the necessities of life in consequence. She said 'Don't talk to me about the pleasures of the common man, or I might tell you something of the sorrows of the common woman, because it's at her expense that he enjoys them.'

Now it was his turn to be impressed. He looked at her, appraisingly, but it was not a judgment on her appearance. There was a recognition of her intelligence and spirit. She asked him 'You're an architect?' 'No', he corrected her, 'I'm a builder.' 'Won't they think it funny to see you fetching and carrying water like this?' He said severely 'There is nothing dishonourable in labour, however hum-

The Uses Of Adversity

ble it may be.' 'Oh yes there is. You should have seen the factory where I worked when I was fourteen. It was dishonourable all right, and so was the reward for it.' He said 'You talk like a socialist.'

She had never thought of herself as a socialist, or indeed as having any political affiliation. But she liked the idea, and was certainly not prepared to deny it. 'What if I am?' she asked, a little defensively, because it was not clear whether he had made his observation as a criticism. It pleased her to think she might have a place in the scheme of things that were generally conceded to be a prerogative of men; that she might be part of some movement, something more than being simply a clever woman, alone and compelled to silence for want of contact with anyone who shared her view of the world. The idea of a struggle for social ends, rather than the effort to survive in the shop and manage the disaster of her marriage, was something she had never articulated; but it certainly existed on the edge of her consciousness. What a relief it would be to see her life, not as a remote site of desolation, but as capable of being linked to some shared activity with people committed to something better – this was what she had been, not seeking exactly, but vaguely anticipating, dreamily in the narrow spaces between her unending labours.

In the days that followed, he returned to the kitchen window, no longer under the pretext of asking for water. She enjoyed the respectful insistence of his approach and the insolence of her own response; the more so since she was at home, while her husband, both *in*valid and inv*a*lid, dozed by the fire, which, he said, his condition demanded, although it was June. The man, framed in the window as though he were a portrait, a Victorian picture of A Working Man, told her his name was Joe. He brought her a copy of Gorge Bernard Shaw's *Intelligent Woman's Guide to Fascism*; and if that prolix socialist condescended in the titles of his polemics, this was not considered at the time to be of significance. Joe gave her *News from Nowhere* by William Morris and a compilation of

Robert Blatchford's *Merrie England*. In return she gave him *David Copperfield* and *Mill on the Floss*. She told him the characters of the aunts in George Eliot's novel were just like those of her own family; that, in any case, Eliot's native Nuneaton was not far from where her own family had come from, Long Buckby, quite close to the Warwickshire border. Her people had the same mournful sensibility and superstitious nature; even their country idiom was similar.

For the first time, she experienced the delight of relationship born of affinity and sympathy, although there was also a strong sexual attraction. She was to deny this later, when she protested that he had been only an instrument in the fulfilment of her project. But that was after he had proved himself as treacherous as the rest of them (did she feel that through Sid she had known all men?)

She did not want to remain childless; and it was with this in mind, she consented that she had consented to meet him in town one evening. Did Sid wonder why she spent so many hours at the kitchen sink? If he did, he said nothing; having, by his own disgrace, forfeited the right to voice any objection to her conduct. Glad didn't hesitate. She would meet Joe the following Tuesday, the day when the shop would be shut. He named a café in the centre of town; a place where women sat in gilt wicker chairs and drank weak coffee at glass-topped tables, and waitresses in black and white with mob-caps always looked as if they were on the point of curtseying to their customers.

With Sid she was irritable, because she was ashamed. Was she not doing the very thing that had brought him to this wretched condition? During the days before the planned meeting, she wondered whether or not she should simply not turn up. It was only by recalling her deeper purpose, she assured me when she at last told her story, that she persuaded herself to keep the appointment.

'Where are you going?' Sid's slow curiosity must have been aroused on the Tuesday morning, when he observed in her an unusual nervous excitement. She tried to force a little dried-up lipstick out of its unused sheath. 'I'm going to meet a friend.' 'Who is he then?' 'No one you know.' 'It is a he then?' 'Not half as heathen as you'. She told him she was going to meet Louie, who had been a bridesmaid at their wedding, 'Bloody horse-godmother' he called her. She had stopped seeing her friends after their marriage. That was more or less expected. 'Friends' were mere make-shifts, people you worked with or had kept contact with after school. They had no place in the circle of kin which closed shut once you were married. Friends were useful only for the small ancillary needs not answered within the confines of the wedded condition and the wider family. In any case, Sid didn't like any of Glad's friends, and that had seemed at the time sufficient proscription for her to renounce them. She began to realise how conventional her behaviour had been; and the irregularity of her position showed her the miserable orthodoxies she had to flout, if she really meant to determine the future course of her life.

Joe was waiting for her outside the café. They sat in a discreet alcove on the first floor, looking down onto the market square. She had never been in such a place. To eat out was an extravagance, and she protested at so much ceremony over something as simple as merely eating. She always expressed an anxiety about the state of the kitchens and the cleanliness of preparation; but her real fear was exposure in a public place, uncertainty as to how to behave. Joe made light of her fears, and ordered a lunch of chicken, peas and new potatoes. She took a glass of red wine which, she said, tasted of rust. She looked critically around her, and wondered that there were in Northampton women with so little to do they had time to dress up in square-shouldered suits, jaunty hats with short veils to show themselves in public with equally idle and frivolous women.

They spent the afternoon together. They sat in the churchyard, where the sun glittered between the splayed green fingers of the horse-chestnut leaves. Crisp furls of holm-oak drifted down. One caught in her hair. He removed them with his fingers and said 'Tell me about your life.'

She had never entered into any such confessional relationship. She spoke cautiously, and said nothing of the reason for her estrangement from Sid; although she made clear that there was neither affection nor any sexual contact between them. 'What about you?' she asked, 'you're married aren't you?' 'How do you know?' 'You have marriage-lines all over your face.' He smiled and told her his wife was an invalid. It was an elective indisposition, but her frailty gave her a reason to withhold from him what, he said, in a refrain she had heard all her adult life, a man needed. She shivered at these words, but they did not deflect her from her purpose. In any case, she really did like him, and could see in him an agreeable companion. He was her intellectual equal, and this suggested new excitements of shared experience she had never dreamed of. She was learning how unreflecting her marriage to Sid had been, how superficial her judgment on what people could give one another, how imprisoning the ascription of the roles of wife and husband. Joe gave her to understand that he was not prepared to jeopardise the security of his wife and home. 'What are you looking for then?' He said 'Friendship.'

And they did become friends. Friendship between men and women unrelated to each other was, of course, prohibited in the streets where she had grown up. The only function of 'outsiders' – the young people you worked with, or with whom you shared a few hours in the park, along the river, going to a dance – was to provide you with a husband or wife. A certain cordiality might be established between the siblings of a potential husband or wife, but friendship with someone of the opposite sex was usually regarded as a screen for less honourable relations.

With Joe she could talk about politics, the war that would soon come, the better world which he did not doubt would triumph. He believed that nothing was too good for the people, and that the real problem with the working class was that it had never asked enough,

The Uses Of Adversity

either of the economic system or of life itself. She wondered whether what the poor need is what the rich have; or whether the violence on which their wealth depended might not also contaminate the poor, should they possess themselves of it? Would wealth itself not become something different, something more noble, if it were more fairly shared? Joe had the reputation of being a Communist. This had cost him jobs; foremen and builders had dismissed him, saying they would make sure he never worked again in this town. But he was also intensely individualistic. He was a skilled craftsman, and had become much in demand in the restoration of churches, which he loved, although he detested the religion which sheltered behind their human-made beauty. He took her to some of the places he had renovated, the weathered gargoyles he had reconstructed from medieval designs, early English tracery he had restored. He said 'Beautiful things do not belong to the rich. Or to God. They belong to the people who created them, the people of England.'

Sid showed all the signs of jealousy. He never knew who she was meeting, and she never spoke about her excursions, which took place every Tuesday. She bought a new coat and shoes, and a black crepe de Chine dress, with crescent moons and stars appliquéd in gold. For the first two months, her meetings with Joe were limited, and she thought, not without a pang of vengeful satisfaction, that it was now Sid's turn to be captive of her desires and design. Let him wonder where she had gone and when, or even whether, she would return. It took a great effort to retrieve feelings that had taken root with Sid. The scars of commitment were still painful. But nothing could be allowed to put at risk what she had come to see as her plan for survival.

After a few weeks, Joe asked her to go away with him to a hotel, where they would spend a night together.

II

She told Sid she was going to stay with her mother, whose seventieth birthday it was. She didn't elaborate, since the act of deception only brought back the feeling that it was she who had been at fault, a conviction that never left her in the presence of Sid's ruin. She had always prided herself on speaking the truth, whatever the consequences. She was compelled to learn yet another bitter lesson, that principles, however elevated, must sometimes be set aside, both to avoid unnecessary pain and also for selfish reasons; and she was determined to have at least one child.

Glad had always tended to moral absolutes and claimed everyone knew right from wrong; but like all truly moral people, she did not let her inflexible rules govern the way she treated others; and, confronted by Sid's trapped helplessness, she melted. 'You'll be all right. I shall be back first thing in the morning.' Incapable of deliberate cruelty, she even regretted her moment of triumph over him. Women, she said, have too much imagination. They know when they are making others suffer, and can anticipate pain, and are therefore less likely willingly to add to it. In any case, she told me, revenge only poisons the victor.

The consummation of what were regarded as illicit relationships had never been easy. The mesh of social life was so dense that there was neither place nor time for them. Industrialism, which in its early stages resembled nothing so much as a military operation, filled every chink and gap in the lives of people. They had to account to someone or other at every moment. They marched to the regimented rhythm of boots on the pavement in the early morning; they moved to the music of bicycle bells as the phalanx of two-wheelers left the factory at dinner-time, and the five-thirty hooter that announced to the whole town that men and women were released from their day's labour. Even pubs, bare, undecorated and

The Uses Of Adversity

functional, had no hiding-place. They were for drinking not dalliance. People went to bed early and rose early. In Northampton town centre, at ten-thirty in the evening, a whistle blew, and the last buses departed. The streets were deserted, and any lone straggler was likely to be interrogated by the police. Even the relaxation of Saturday night was highly ritualised, when the men took too much beer and the women had to undress them, put them to bed and prevent them from urinating in the wardrobe. Sunday morning was set aside for sex; but the way wives alluded to it when they had reached a certain age suggested an unwilling submission, even a martyrdom which for them, at least, brought no enjoyment. It was difficult to know whether they were expressing an inbred Puritanism about the sins of the flesh, whether they were truly revolted, or whether they might be tempting fate if they admitted to any pleasure.

But the texture of social life was imporous, designed to prevent anyone from breaching its sturdy fabric and wandering into the pathless realms beyond. Any departure of behaviour from recognised norms was liable to comment and censure. The working class culture was, moreover, a formidable matchmaker; people married as a result of their physical propinquity, the children of neighbours or workmates; and despite a theoretical taboo on pre-marital sex, shotgun weddings were so familiar that this had, by the nineteen fifties, before a prohibition that had outlived its usefulness. Almost interchangeable, not much store was set on a 'choice' of partners. It was said there were more fish in the sea than ever came out of it; a metaphor that pre-dated the exhaustion of coastal waters by mechanised trawlers. Anyone who looked far afield for a purpose as simple as selecting a life-partner (for what became for many, a life-sentence) was considered unnecessarily choosy or was thought to have something to hide; and no good was predicted to come of such unions.

This was, of course, the other side of the much praised – and widely disputed – ideal of community. It was indeed warm and embracing, and it did bear people up at times of sorrow and loss; but only as long as they abided by its behavioural prescriptions. It involved a heavily policed form of caring. In the street where one of my aunts lived, a man shared a house with his wife and a woman believed to be her sister. It was not until it became known (how? – things became known only in defiance of unofficial secrets acts) that the sister was sister in only the most general sense of the word, that the community ostracised them. It seemed he had married both of them; and rather than admit to a bigamous attachment, they had, in anticipation of a time to come they could not foresee, opted to share him. On the other hand, the community was capable of acts of charitable indulgence, provided that ambiguities remained and relationships remained in shadow. Eddie, our neighbour's son who claimed his mother was his only sweetheart, sometimes went fishing or birds'-nesting with a fifteen-year old, whose father had died. This was not, at that time, regarded as grounds for suspicion of deviancy, but the actions of a man, himself lonely, who enjoyed the company of youngsters. They could be seen beside the river, placidly watching the floats in the water, scarcely exchanging a few words during the whole day. When people saw them, they would say with serene approbation, 'There goes Eddie with young Jim for a day's fishing.'

III

At that time, any couple who appeared in a hotel would be immediately suspect. Only commercial travellers and theatricals put up in hotels; and there were a few establishments for this purpose, close to the cattle market. They exuded an air of pinched disreputability, landladies with hairnets and scarlet nails, suggested connivance at

The Uses Of Adversity

lubricious nights to come. Any man and woman not sleeping at home would clearly be thought adulterous. For this reason, on the Saturday they were to meet, Joe thought it better if they avoided the embarrassment of presenting themselves to public scrutiny. Joe had an Austin Seven, and since it was a fine warm day in late summer, he drove deep into the countryside. He parked the car in a gateway, where a broken wooden gate and the hedgerows were overgrown with convolvulus, travellers' joy and ripe blackberries. They followed the margin of the field, and flattened a space about twenty yards from the edge of the ripe wheat. This shocked Glad, who remembered from her childhood that it was a crime to trample growing crops. He spread a rug on the pale wheatstalks; some rabbits ran away in a flash of white tails. Late corn poppies lent their silky redness to the afternoon. Glad was tense, as much from being in the open air and at risk of discovery, as from any scruple about what she was doing. There was no one in sight; in the warmth and stillness of the afternoon, they made love. For Joe it was a great release; his wife had refused to let him touch her for more than two years. Glad was taken aback by the vehemence of his approach. She had told him nothing about Sid's condition; only that their marriage had broken down.

She wanted desperately to conceive. In her eagerness, she responded to Joe with an abandon that he misunderstood. He thought he discerned a passion for himself in an enthusiasm that had its roots in causes about which he knew nothing. He could readily understand (what man can't?) that she might be seduced by his unusual mixture of charm and radicalism, and was not displeased; although he might have been uneasy about the difficulties that might arise, should he want to extricate himself from the relationship. She said 'He needn't have worried.' He assumed control, and, like all the men who knew her, underestimated her depth, her intelligence and powers of persistence.

She was attracted to him; but this had to be subordinated to her own plan. He had strayed unmindfully into her life, a character from a quite different tale, a random though providential actor; and quite unaware of his role. In this way, the relationship began as an exercise in mutual deception, which may have undermined any possibility that it would develop into a more lasting attachment. She was trying to salvage something from the ruin of her marriage, and Joe was a shadowy, if vital, part of it. She remained lonely and preoccupied, even when she appeared at her most earnestly involved. She did not dwell upon what he felt or thought. She said she wondered, briefly, whether he might perhaps be persuaded to leave his wife and live with her; but she soon understood that his radicalism was destined to remain in the realm of theory, and, in any case, it did not extend to sexual emancipation. He was obviously waiting for the better world that would undoubtedly come; when relationships between men and women would become more open and free; and such a time would occur, almost certainly in their lifetime. This she interpreted as a declaration that he intended to do nothing to alter the comfortable misery of his present life.

He was, if anything, more furtively anxious about being discovered than she was. Hopes of fulfilling her design gave her a certain recklessness. For a few weeks, they met frequently on Saturday evenings. She awaited with interest a change in the weather which would prevent their visits to cornfields. In any case, the harvest was almost finished. Glad looked on the stubble which shone like glass, and she remembered the times when she had gone gleaning with her mother, the ears of corn collecting in her apron, no longer for grinding and making bread as it used to be in her grandmother's time, but for feeding the hens.

One Saturday it was raining. They checked into a country pub, saying they had come for the wedding of relatives. The woman behind the desk asked if it was for Mr Selby and Miss Roberts, since that was the only wedding scheduled for the following day. Yes, yes, she had said. No one demanded to see the wedding invitation, and

The Uses Of Adversity

nobody said Mr Selby would be coming in for a drink a bit later. It was all easy. Joe told her she had read too many stories in the Sunday papers about the hiring of private detectives and professional co-respondents. One day they had made love in the car, which Joe had parked as far he could drive it down a muddy path into a beechwood. It was uncomfortable, and afterwards, they became irritable with each other. The wheels got stuck in the channel they had made, and she had to find brushwood to help the car move, and then together they pushed it back towards the road.

Within three months of their first meeting she was pregnant. Telling Joe was easy; she relished it less than she would enjoy telling Sid. She had assured Joe that it was safe each time they had made love, which was far from the truth. He was angry and his view of their future association was clearly challenged by the new circumstances. He had foreseen a relationship that would continue without disturbing his marriage. One afternoon, they sat in the garden of a country pub in tense silence. It was September. The harvest was finished. The berries of hawthorn and elder hung in red and black clusters in the hedgerows. He thought he had been tricked, which, of course, he had; but not in the way he imagined. She said 'I don't want anything from you. I shan't ask for money.' 'There's no need to have babies these days. I mean, you're not an ignorant shop-girl.' She said 'You don't seem to have much respect for the people you're going to raise up. Anyway, I am a shop-girl. Not so ignorant perhaps.' This time, they made no arrangement to meet again.

Did he think she wanted to force him into divorce and marriage with her? She felt humiliated that he should interpret her behaviour in this way, although in view of the sparseness of the information she had given him about her situation, this was bound to be his interpretation. She wanted to tell him the truth – that what she had done bore no relation to him beyond his purely biological function. But that wasn't the truth either. In any case, if she had said any such thing to him, he would not have believed her, and would have been humiliated in his turn. She preferred to let him think of her as a woman scheming to detach him from his wife. As it happened, she felt compassion for the wife, who had – for whatever reason – been unable to take pleasure in his body as she had. At one point, Joe had said something about his wife's tender friendship with a female cousin, and seemed on the verge of some disclosure, but then had thought better of it.

What had not entered her calculations was the sadness that would engulf her as soon as what she saw as her purpose had been accomplished. The man she had thought was only instrumental in her plan, had somehow found a way through her defensive obsession in spite of herself. The feeling was like a superficial wound, which you scarcely notice at the time, until it wakes you in the night with a deeper ache.

IV

When she got home that Saturday evening, she found Sid sprawled in the armchair. He had kicked off his shoes, and fallen asleep listening to some racing commentary. His socks had potatoes in them; she no longer darned them. By the time she came in, the radio was playing dance music. She looked at him and felt a pang of tenderness. The knowledge that life was within her made her happy, and she saw herself as attached to all living things. She saw how completely Sid was at her mercy; but perhaps no more so than she had been at his. This did not gratify her. She did not want so much power over him. She had looked forward to the moment when she would tell him she was pregnant. She would punish him for what she could now reasonably claim was his inability to create life within her. The miscarriages had not perhaps been a result of some physical defect in her. Then she thought of the sterile waste of

The Uses Of Adversity

his substance with all the women he had known, and the disease that ravaged him, while she was so vital and full of energy. Her moment of pity gave way to a feeling of exhaustion – how complicated and full of effort it had been to achieve what most women took for granted. So much scheming for what ought to have been natural and spontaneous. Here was distinction indeed; but it brought her no comfort.

She made tea, and as she set his cup down beside him, he looked up at her, yawned, and as though he had momentarily forgotten what lay between them, smiled spontaneously, stretching his arms. She could not see his face, because the late sunlight that came through the west-facing window obscured his expression. 'Sid my duck', she began, using the dialect endearment with him for the first time in years. He stirred and sat up. 'I've got something to tell you.' He looked at her attentively; the moment had become ceremonious, a profane annunciation. She said 'I'm pregnant.'

He looked at her, a look she could not see but felt; rage, disbelief, impotence. 'You can't be.' But he knew she would not lie about such things. He felt he ought to protest. He owed it...to what, exactly? The pride of his gender? His vanished supremacy? His assertiveness as male head of household? He quickly realised how ridiculous that would be. That she had accepted far worse from him gave him small comfort. He said, choosing his words with unfamiliar care, 'Who does it belong to?' 'Me,' she said. 'Go on', he replied, half joking, 'even you couldn't do it all by yourself.'

She was calm as she prepared the meal, which they ate in silence. He would not look at her. She felt that she had only added to their sufferings, and for a moment entertained a wild idea that she would have an abortion, devote herself to her sick husband, try to undo the harm that had been done. The silence was broken only by the sound of knife and fork on the willow-patterned plates, the crunch of cucumber, the stirring of tea. She knew that the journey on which she had embarked was irreversible. She had to prepare herself for what would follow. When they had finished, she pushed her plate away and said, not unkindly, 'Listen Sid, and I'll tell you what I want you to do. You know and I know that we were never going to have children after this. But nobody outside these walls knows that. I want you to say it is yours.'

'Never. You've been carrying on with some bloke, and you expect me, not only to close my eyes to it, but claim paternity of his bastard.', he said with the air of one to whom all deception is abhorrent. 'You should hear yourself.' 'What if I won't do it?'

'Sid.' Glad spoke softly. 'Who he might be is neither here nor there. It really doesn't matter. It was not him I wanted, it was a baby. I'm nearly thirty five. If we'd had our own, it would have been different. But that can't happen now. And it isn't my fault, as you'll see, if everything goes as I think it will. But I'm going to have this baby, and you will have to say it's yours. No', she corrected herself. 'You don't need to do that. All you have to do is not deny it. You'll do it because you have no option. You haven't. You threw choice away a long time ago. I shan't ask anything of you. I shan't expect you to maintain it. I don't want money. I can earn. I'll get someone to help in the shop when the baby is due. After that, we'll carry on as we agreed. I shall look after you, do whatever is necessary until you are cured. Then we'll separate. It doesn't have to be made more difficult than it is.'

She hated the sound of her own voice, as she delivered this rehearsed ultimatum; it was constricted and forced. It did not represent how she felt. Sick with anxiety, she was revolted by herself; and only the thought of the alternative drove her on. Sid fell into a sulk. He smoked half a packet of cigarettes, and told her to do what she thought best. He would not interfere with her plans.

Only when she went upstairs that night, passing her body into the cold envelope of the sheets on the big double bed, she let go and wept. Although everything she had intended was resolving itself more or less as she had intended, it brought her neither peace nor satisfaction. But neither of these things had ever been vouchsafed her. Her temperament and sensibility were at odds, not only with the social order, but, it seemed to her, with life itself. Even when she had achieved what she wanted, the manner of its accomplishment and the manner in which it had been attained, robbed her of any sense of victory. She consoled herself that she was more than a match for these men whom chance had determined would play such significant roles in her life; but it was a sad, stale triumph.

V

She had twins, who were born in the maternity home endowed by and named after one of the principal shoe families in the town. Sid found himself the recipient of congratulations from family as well as strangers, which he bore with a stoicism he had certainly not exhibited in any other aspect of his life. When people looked at my brother or me and said we were the image of him, he liked the idea of this surrogate paternity. This was not to say that he had any intention of playing any part in our upbringing, even if such an opportunity were offered him. Soon after we were born, he started again to go out in the evenings. He was kept apart from us completely, and this, together with his wife's rejection, made him a lonely and superfluous figure in the house. He was never allowed to pick us up, to kiss, or even touch us, ostensibly because of the (unlikely) risk of infection. She could not have anticipated that his emphatic exile only lent – to me at least – an aura of unattainable romance to his gender. He began to put on weight, and at length his skin assumed the chalky consistency of that untouched by loving hands. Long before he was declared cured, his erotic vagrancy was resumed; and she made no effort to stop him; although she asked him to think of the women his wanderlust (literally) would put at risk. She preferred to be alone with us, and to recount in sighing monologues the injustices of life and the iniquities of men.

Joe, also childless, had no access to us either. After a period of withdrawal over what he described as her 'treachery', he contacted her again. They met a few times in town. He wanted to renew their sexual relationship. She refused, even though for her he had lost nothing of his attractiveness. She had to prove to him that her pregnancy had not been a stratagem to make him leave his wife, or to obtain maintenance money from him. In any case, she had become so locked into her own purposes, and had persuaded herself that he, too, would also abandon her; so she made up her mind to keep him at a distance. As the time to give birth approached, his demeanour towards her changed. He seemed to take pride in a fatherhood he could not claim, and which he had repudiated in advance. When we were born, he even became jealous of Sid; it would be difficult to conceive of a more inappropriate emotion. He protested and wept and, aggrieved, he declared she had no right to keep him from his boys. She said 'You said you wanted nothing to do with them, and that is what you'll get. Just see whether or not I can manage on my own.' It was bitter to say these words, but her pride forbade her to depend upon him for anything.

Twins were a misfortune in more than one respect. It was not simply that this added to her already overwhelming burden of labour; but my mother's life had been dominated by men who came in twos; characterised by a strange dualism, opposites of good and evil, honest and dishonourable, fair and foul. Her brothers were either 'wrong'uns' or 'good men'. To the former category belonged those who had shown strength of will, which indeed did often manifest itself in bullying or violent behaviour; while to the latter those who had been more pliable, amenable to being managed. Harry and Joe were wrong'uns, since Harry had permitted his mother to expend every last ounce of her physical energy waiting on him; even when she was weakened by age, he came home from

The Uses Of Adversity

work and lifted his boots to her apron, so that she would untie and remove them. And Joe, who had lost an arm and a leg in the First World War, was an unhappy man, who had once had a fight outside a pub with another war amputee, also with one leg, who agreed to have one of his sound hands tied behind his back in order to fight fair; Joe's only son killed himself. In contrast to these was Dick, a self-taught intellectual, a union official, a thoughtful and gentle man, a resource to the boot and shoe workers, to whose many grievances, unfair dismissals, illnesses, unhappiness he ministered. Her sister Win's boy, Reg, was also a good man. He had come home on leave during the war, and, revolted by the brutality of what he had witnessed, he refused to go back. He asked Glad if he could stay with her so that when the military police came for him, they wouldn't find him. She said to him 'No, duck, I can't do that.' In any case, there was no room in the house. He returned to his mother's house, was duly apprehended by the military police, was sent to North Africa, where he was killed almost immediately. She regretted she had been unable to shelter him, and accused herself of being partly responsible for his death.

Her brothers-in-law occupied a similarly Manichean position. Frank, the responsible, mature invalid husband of Aunt Em, who spent his whole life devoted to her welfare when he would be gone. He was agreed by everyone to have been 'a saint' a designation never to be bestowed on any man in robust health. The elevation of his status was directly proportionate to his incapacity to do harm. On the other hand, Arthur was consigned, however unfairly, to the 'wrong'uns, a man whose principal failing seems to have been his obsessive espousal of a racism that was, at that time, a little too close to that of the enemies of Britain for comfort.

In this taxonomy of good and evil, the good were those who displayed features as little associated with working class males as possible, and the bad exhibited all the qualities of the stereotypes, the boozers and gamblers, the despisers of women, upon whom they remained, however, childishly dependent.

She said 'Not all men were like our father. When he came in from work, she'd rush to pick up the things he dropped on the floor. If any of the children were sitting in his chair, they'd have to be out of it before he came through the door. And if his dinner didn't please him – she might have had nothing but a ham-bone and some potatoes – he'd take up the plate and throw it against the wall. Our walls were always marked by dinners that had incurred his displeasure…Women were intermediaries between children and their fathers. Whenever he raised his hand to any of us, she would put herself between his hand and our body, so more often than not she'd catch the edge of the blow across her own face. When he was at home, he demanded and got the best of everything. He was master. At work it was different. There, he was nothing. They were humiliated in the factory. He vented his anger on us. I suppose it gave him satisfaction to see his wife suffer. It put her in the same boat he was in most of the time.

'I realised that not everybody lived in the same way. Some men were temperance and went to chapel, but they were a minority. They might dig their bit of allotment, grow carrots and onions, even tend some dahlias for the town show. But they were thought to as a bit of Mary-Ann, not how you wanted your boys to be. My older brothers followed their Dad. They'd swagger off down the road, daring each other to swim in the river with no clothes on, fetching rats out of the ditches, and treating the girls the way they meant to go on – making them cry.'

When my brother and I were born, the temptation to brand us in accordance with these stereotypes must have strong. At least, she did not damn one of us from birth. Instead, she behaved as at a fairy-tale christening, where virtues are bestowed on the newly born; an event invariably spoiled, when the uninvited witch distributes evil characteristics to the innocent babes. I was given her restless and insomniac sensibility, and I cried ceaselessly. My brother, placid and obedient, slept all the time. Because I resembled her so closely, to have made me into a villain would have been to condemn herself. So she hit upon the (for her) happy expedient of assuring each of us separately that he was the good one, while confiding to each the badness of the other; with the result that we both grew up believing ourselves to be the good twin, and the brother a source of unspeakable pain and worry to her.

VI

In other words, my brother and I were separated at birth, even though we lived together in the same house for the first eighteen years of our lives. The circumstances of our birth impelled our mother to do everything within her considerable power to keep us apart. Our mutual estrangement, exacerbated by time, lasted until his death in 2005. Even then, I heard that he had died only indirectly, since there had been no communication between us since our mother's funeral, fifteen years earlier.

I can scarcely believe these words, even as I write them. How could we have grown in such physical closeness, and yet have behaved towards each other as if were strangers? It was worse than being strangers, for we had been familiar figures in each other's life from the start. A deep temperamental difference divided us; and this was reinforced, both by the determination of a powerful woman, and by a social system hat supported separation. Our mother had skilfully managed the state of impassive hostility that kept us apart; we lived in a state of frozen kinship. Nothing passed between us, because our lives were both turned towards our mother.

There was a tangle of secrets to be kept: syphilis, adultery, illegitimacy were not the objects of social indifference they have become. To have kept them for so many years must have been an unimaginable burden; and although she confided in Aunt May, her sister was no benign comforter, since, although loyal and silent as the grave, she did not believe that wrongdoing should escape the torments of conscience it deserved; and accordingly she appointed herself elective avenging angel.

Was it Glad's own necessary secretiveness that made her insist her children tell her everything, withhold nothing from her, since if they did, they would surely be found out? Sometimes she would say 'There is nothing I don't know', and she turned her grim stone-grey eyes upon us, in which we saw reflected in her omniscience our own diminished image, our guilt and shame. She extracted from us promises of constancy which the men in her life had failed to sustain.

Her principal concern, especially during her pregnancy and in our early years, was to make sure Sid and Joe would never meet. Our biological father, still aggrieved by what he regarded as her wiles, offered nothing to our upkeep, which she had assured him she would refuse. Who can say what menacing future she foresaw, if her twin boys should combine against her, conspire for her ruin, when one man had deserted her for a sexually transmitted disease, and the other had abandoned her to the consequences of what he thought was her own lack of foresight?

No encounter ever took places between our joint fathers; and there was never any real meeting between their divided children. Later, as we grew up, Joe did occasionally make an appearance in our lives. At such times, unaccountably lachrymose and tender, he would question us closely about our ambition, what we wanted to do when we left school – a state so unimaginably distant at the time that it was difficult to formulate any answer at all. We resented what we saw as the intrusive enquiries of a stranger. He had grown fatter and his moustache was yellowed by nicotine. He wore pepper-and-salt tweeds and good quality brogues. The question of the

The Uses Of Adversity

place he thought he occupied in our lives we did not, of course ask; but I was darkly conscious of the impropriety of the irruption of a stranger into these intimate spaces. I detected the tension between him and our mother, but if there had been any connection between them, it could not have been very substantial, since she belonged emphatically to us. Our mother had relations – there were plenty of those – but apart from with her children, relationships were unseaworthy vessels at best. She sat with clenched pride, asking nothing of him, even when her purse was depleted and the succession of men who came to help cut up the meat were helping themselves to money from the till. She was frugal and sparing and spent nothing on herself. Nothing was too good for us, except the one thing we might have valued above all else, the sweetness of one another's companionship.

Our mother watched us all the time. One day when we were about four, we were giggling in the corner over some trivial amusement. She parted us roughly, precisely because we were not quarrelling. We were puzzled by her anger. In the division of labour already marked out for us, she told me to go and look at a book and my brother to play with the dog.

The allocation of roles between us multiplied, physically and psychically. I was clever, but he was beautiful. No more malign separation could have been devised. It was decided that I would rise socially and my brother would break hearts; that her own might be the first to be shattered did not enter her calculations. Her efforts to keep us apart were strengthened by circumstances which, in the 1940s and 50s, made it possible for my brother and me to be assigned to different social classes, a fact which continued to bewilder and pain me every day of my life, never more so than now he is dead. This was made easier by the fact that we shared only one thing in common – apart from our unavowed parentage – and that was an introversion, which made communication between us all the more difficult. I do not know how desperate his desire was for the thwarted fraternal relationship I longed for.

He slept in a room of his own from the age of six, while I continued to share a room – the abandoned conjugal chamber – with my mother. I was frightened of the dark, of shadows, of dreams, of death, or perhaps, simply of the mysteries which emerged with the night from their caves and hovered over us – the secret of our birth, Sid's transgressive sickness, the abstract paternity we could not identify, the intermittent and arbitrary appearance of Joe, and the admonition that we would know – wisdom more potent for being unspecified – when we hadn't got her.

She policed our growth and development, anticipating by many years the maleness which she would have stopped in its course. When I was eight, I was getting undressed to have my nightly wash by the fire. She took my underpants, inspected them and sniffed. 'What's this?' she asked sharply, indicating a small stain at the crotch. 'It's wee-wee', I said, puzzled by the vehemence of her tone. 'What else could it be?' 'Never you mind', she answered with an air of mystery. I wondered what strange emission from my body could have created such suspicion, and it hinted at a future source of shame, which would unfold in a future gravid with even more extreme anxieties than I already knew.

VII

Sid continued to occupy the spare room, the damp prohibited chamber which mingled maleness and mildew with disease and smoke. It exercised a fateful lure, and sometimes I cast a fearful glance at the disorder within – the dingy bedclothes thrown back to reveal the mysterious hollow in which his forbidden body slept, the blot of mould on the wall, a smell which I later identified as semen, all of which combined to furnish me with early fantasies of the

The Uses Of Adversity

stranger who embodied this intimate absence of fatherhood. I had erotic dreams about him, which induced a further – and wholly unnecessary – sense of guilt, since in the end, he proved to have been no blood connection, related to us, as it were, only by marriage. During the war, when he had somewhat negligently officiated as Air Protection Warden in bomb shelters, young women in the neighbourhood were drawn by the strong resemblance he was said to have borne to Henry Fonda.

Gladys rigorously monitored the slow, even stunted, unfolding of our gender, which she would have preferred us to abjure, as though we were citizens of a country overrun by tyranny. Our childhood was pervaded by her mute but eloquent entreaty that if time rendered adulthood inevitable, we should at least strive to be as little as possible like the men who had wronged her. This had a serious effect upon my brother, whose emotional and sexual development was impaired by her disapproval; whereas, since I was gay, the prohibition on masculine identity came as no conscious sacrifice, since I was content to seek it in others. This, of course, was the object of another taboo, and appeared to supply me with secrets almost as dreadful as hers.

In our town there must have been at least two or three thousand people at least who preferred same-sex relationships, and some no doubt remained celibate. But Northampton, like all towns and cities in puritanical industrial Britain, had its own transgressive spaces, which were set aside, vacant sites for sexual irregularity. This was a park on the edge of town, which also extended into the central area. It was a dark fragment of countryside, a place apart, where adultery could be safely 'committed', and extra-marital relationships might find brief and uncomfortable accommodation.

This parkland sloped down towards the flood plain of the river, where the open-air swimming-pool was established; an attraction for gay men, although neither they nor anyone else at that time attributed to them that cheerful designation. There was always something erotic about swimming-pools: people made holes in the partitions between changing areas to spy on those in the next cubicle. It was also the only place in Northampton where almost-naked bodies were on display, even if still innocent of tans and creams, burnt bright red by a spell of summer sunshine. I was aware of the park as a place of forbidden sexuality, and I feared what I might discover about myself if I ventured into its inviting recesses.

I was later to learn much about this site of shadowy impropriety. My mother's eldest sister had a daughter, Hilda, who was only two or three years younger than my mother. She told me this story shortly before she died in 1987. Hilda rarely attended school, because her mother kept her at home in defiance of threatening School Board authorities, as both company and servant for herself. It was her job to run with sixpences to place bets on a horse her mother fancied, to fetch a jug of stout from the off-licence, as well as to wash and clean the house. When she was fourteen, truanting from her labour, Hilda had gone one late afternoon for a walk in this park. It was always deserted, for those who availed themselves of its privacy kept themselves well hidden by bushes and long grass. It was devoid of public attractions, except the occasional fun-fair, where dangerous men with swarthy faces and gold teeth set up dodgems and carousels, and tried to seduce teenage girls with candyfloss and promises of a good time. In Northampton, they perhaps discovered, time was not meant to be good. It was something to be got through, stoically and without complaint.

As Hilda was walking, dusk fell, and it was almost dark before she reached the main road. She was suddenly seized from behind. A man dragged her into the bushes. He put a hand over her mouth and told her he would slit her throat if she screamed. She said 'He did what he had to do, and left me on the gravel.' Her words were significant: she spoke with fatalism as though this were an irresistible male compulsion, as though she had been overcome by a force of nature, and her status as victim was incidental. Traumatised and bleeding, she cleaned herself in the river, and when she reached home, she was punished by her mother for being late. I asked her 'Did you know who he was?' She said 'No. But I saw him around town for years afterwards. He didn't recognise me, but I never forgot him.' I said 'Why didn't you tell anyone?' She said 'I thought it was my fault. It was my fault. Everybody knew what went on in the park. You didn't go down there unless you were looking for trouble. I asked for it and I got it.'

VIII

Separation became something of an obsession for me. The complete isolation from my twin was accompanied by a morbid fear of separation from my mother. For the first few years of my life, I could not bear to lose sight of her. Whenever she was swallowed up by the closing of a door, or by the switch of a light, I howled until her presence was restored. I can see now that the loss of my brother as a kind of bereavement. I compensated for his absence by an excessive attachment to my mother. The severed twin was always present but never visible.

My dependency on my mother, and my terror of losing her, set up other pathologies. Her departure (or death, which seemed a more likely agent of her disappearance) was the most frightful event I could imagine; and accordingly, I never ceased imagining it. I came early to the comfortless conclusion that it would be folly ever to permit myself any other relationship, since this must also involve the same intolerable abridgement I anticipated from this one. All my feelings were locked in the airless chamber of my devotion to her, and I was incapable of permitting myself any other involvement, least of all with the brother whose extinguished presence remained as inert to me as that of the kitchen table or the broom-cupboard.

For a long time, I didn't recognise the origin of what later seemed to me an incapacity to feel for others. I found refuge in dwelling upon the suffering of humanity in general, the brevity of life, the certainty of death, but this was the only way I could find expression for the choked feelings of a dependency that had little to do with love, but everything to do with a fear of loss. I was well into my thirties before I knew the meaning of a mutual loving relationship with another adult. Because irreparable loss is inscribed in every deep commitment to another, I thought it better to stay away from them. And I did.

My brother may well have experienced something similar; but since we never discussed such things, it is impossible to know. It may have been worse for him, because he did not so readily yield to our mother's demand for unconditional surrender to her better knowledge of everything. If I had the misfortune to resemble her, he had the greater disadvantage of having to resist her invasive power. She could not tie him to herself as she so effortlessly bound me. She therefore paid him more attention than I ever received, despite the clamour and fuss I made; this was unwelcome and oppressive to him. It also led him to the (mistaken) belief that she cared more for me than for him; and I alone knew that the opposite was the truth. I was a pushover, he was a challenge. Her attempts to win him over were evidence of a preference which he could not be expected to discern. I was jealous of his difference from her, and of his ability to create inner defences. He looked at her from within the impregnable citadel of his own heart, and she resented an independence which I coveted but could never hope to attain. I would love to have loved, but there was nothing left in the depleted account of my feelings to spend on him.

I failed him in many ways, and some of these I can trace to precise occasions. One day, when we were still in primary school, he fell ill and had to be taken home. Mrs Wrench told me I need not

The Uses Of Adversity

return that day after I had taken my brother home. I begged that someone else might accompany him, since I had no wish to miss the lesson. I felt particularly virtuous in this request, and if the teacher gave me a strange look of pity and puzzlement, its meaning became clear to me only much later. On another occasion, walking home from school, he had what was politely called an 'accident'. Suffering from diarrhoea, he stood still on the path, his leg smeared with shit. Appalled, I ran home to tell our mother what had happened. She closed the shop and went back to meet him, while I sat on the grass and immersed myself in Sunny Stories. She gathered some dock leaves from the hedgerow, wiped him clean and brought him back, consoling him, no doubt, by drawing his attention to my flight from the scene of his embarrassment and shame, and assuring him she could be trusted never to do so.

I was convinced that my brother brought nothing but trouble and unhappiness to her. That was, I assumed, why she never ceased worrying about him and why she chose me as her confidant. On the day her own mother died, in November 1948, I was in bed with one of the many unidentified sicknesses that scarred my childhood. She came upstairs and leaned over the bed, her eyes dark with misery and cheeks stained with tears. 'What's the matter?' I asked with all the solicitous sagacity of my nine years, 'Is it him?'

In order to account to my brother for her yielding to the constant demands I made, she would say 'Well, you know what he's like', so that he came to understand that my wayward intractability was the source of her constant suffering. She was insecure, so frightened of disclosure of her secrets that she developed a conspiratorial complicity with each of us against the other. She betrayed us all the time, in order to prevent us from betraying her.

This engineering of our divided destinies did not arise as deliberate plan; it was scarcely conscious at all. It was a malign consequence of an overwhelming and expiatory love, of the nature of which its objects have no conception. She felt guilt that she had brought into the world two illegitimate children, at a time when such children still bore that stigma; and the word bastard was something more than a semi-affectionate term denoting fellow-feeling, as in poor bastard, or lucky bastard. Enough people had some inkling of her secret for its inevitable disclosure at some point. Since the bitterest wounds are always inflicted by loving hands, she was convinced that everything she did was for the best, or at least our own good. Her work of separation was not intentional, and she would have been shocked if anyone had pointed out its effects. But there no one was to do so. The most that was ever said of me and my brother was that we were chalk and cheese; though which of these substances each of us resembled remained unspoken.

Our mother might have spared herself some of the trouble she took to keep us apart. The social arrangements which would assist her in her work of separation were at hand. At eleven he went to the Secondary Modern School, a holding centre for the stigmatised youngsters of an estate known as Windy Ridge, into which former slum-dwellers had been decanted. While he struggled in the C-stream (against teachers and their low expectations, against the other kids and the punitive atmosphere of those certified to have failed in advance), I raced through my studies, and soon learned to accept all the wonderful qualities which a new meritocracy claimed to have discerned in me. My brother was said to be 'good with his hands'; but everyone knew this was a euphemism for not being a scholar, and as such, a humiliating consolation prize. He came home with objects he had crafted, a wooden stool, a small chest of drawers on which he had lavished his considerable creative powers; our mother kept the little chest beside her chair for the rest of her life, when it became a small shrine to him. When she died, we found it contained some of his rare letters to her from his time in the army in Germany, his wedding photographs and pictures of his children as infants.

The Uses Of Adversity

Largely self-taught, Gladys had an idolatrous veneration for formal education. My brother's inability to avail himself of this facility was the source of perhaps the most significant rift between us. She also sought, hesitantly and not very successfully, to cultivate in us a taste for the arts in her obscure yearning for a better life that went beyond the material. This meant being allowed to stay up late on Sunday evenings, to listen to a concert of light classics on the radio, called Grand Hotel, which, introduced by Strauss's *Roses from the South*, broadcast the voices of sopranos singing from the *Merry Widow* or *White Horse Inn*. She also read to us from her favourite book, *Bleak House*, which seemed to us largely meteorological in content, about fog in London and incessant rain in Lincolnshire.

My brother left school at fifteen to be apprenticed to a carpenter and joiner. This position had been secured for him by Joe, who knew the best master-craftsmen in the town, and thought this was the least he could do for his unacknowledged son. My brother came home shedding pale wood shavings and exuding a resinous scent of distant pine-forests. He would leave the house every morning on his bicycle, with a tin box of sandwiches and an apple, skidding in the icy February dawn, while I remained in bed, luxuriating in the prospect of further adventures in the subjunctive of French verbs. He worked diligently and uncomplainingly, and duly acquired artisanal skills that were becoming rare in an era of mechanisation. Once, when he had been detained for prolonged and unpaid overtime, our mother went to the workshop and told his boss that if he thought he could exploit a boy because he had no father to stand up for him, he had another think coming, because she was as capable of defending him as any man. The boss said something to his apprentice about your mother being a bit of a Tartar; but from that time, he always announced overtime in advance, and paid him for it. Our mother often said to us that she had had to be both father and mother to us; and I sometimes wondered at the ease with which she could pass in and out of genders, when I had such difficulty in establishing a precarious corner in just one of them.

In his spare time, my brother made model aeroplanes with balsa wood, covered with tissue paper and stuck together with a glue which had the effect of inducing a faint euphoria which no one at the time was able to trace the source of.

VIII

I later learned from friends that this form of social segregation within families as not uncommon. At least two classmates had gone to Grammar School, only to see a brother and sister extradited, protesting, to the tyranny of the local Secondary. This had also set up rivalries and resentments that were to last throughout their lives. At the time, these showed themselves as challenges about talking posh and using big words nobody could understand; about spending all their time stuck in a book and not going out with other kids, scrumping, breaking windows and tormenting eccentrics on the estate; or about being so weedy and showing a nancy-ish aversion to sport. Quite a few of my contemporaries were divided from siblings by an education that directed some to a professional or academic career and others to manual or 'low-grade' clerical work. None of them, however, experienced the absolute break that took place between me and my brother.

As an adolescent, my twin went out regularly for Sunday evening cycle rides with Uncle Alec, husband of my mother's eldest sister. He was a gaunt, taciturn man, dominated by his wastrel wife, whose noisy hedonism was so shockingly at variance with the sepulchral sensibility of her sisters. Lill drank copiously, loved the theatre, especially melodrama, and only stirred from her fireside to attend the occasional race meeting. Inactivity evidently made her

The Uses Of Adversity

feel the cold, to such an extent that one day she burned the house down by an indiscriminate use of paraffin to encourage the fire to burn.

Alec took his nephew to visit country churches, where they admired medieval misericordes and half-obliterated wall-paintings. They would drink lemonade outside pubs, to the melancholy accompaniment of church bells and acrid autumn bonfires. I was incredulous at this unlikely friendship which had so small a dependency on words for communication. Perhaps their attachment came from a tacit understanding that both were victims of powerful women in the family. I once came across Alec with our mother, in the kitchen. She was all flustered and blushing, and he was saying 'Come on Glad, you're a bit of all right, you are. You're the one I should have had.' It later became clear that this was not quite the dramatic confession it appeared to be, since he had worked his way through the sisters of his wife and had had some sort of relationship with at least two of them, excluding the one to whom he was officially wedded. It occurred to me that if Uncle Alec was so assiduous in seeking out the lustreless company of my brother, this was probably a pretext that would open the way to our mother; I was obscurely comforted by the thought, since I knew that the path to that particular destination was beset by obstacles not easily surmounted.

Once, my brother tried to talk with me about sex. By then – we were about fifteen – I knew much about the mechanics of sex, but I could not imagine sharing with him what I knew in general, and even less what I suspected about myself. I now realise he made a number of oblique pleas to me when we were adolescent. If I rebuffed them, this was because I did not recognise them for what they were. I regarded them as an encroachment on the slim margin of autonomy that remained after my mother, an imperial power, had annexed all the territory around her, and the fragment of uncolonised ground on which I stood threatened to collapse at any moment.

At eighteen, he was 'called up' into the army; a significant verb, since all his life he had been called up by others. Our very birth had been a summons from our mother to relieve her of her own isolation and wretchedness. My brother was posted to Germany while I was still in the VI form, acting with my friends in plays, for which we hired the Co-Op Hall, and discussing the iniquities of Suez and the meaning of the Hungarian uprising against the Soviet Union. I took it as no more than due recognition that I would go to Cambridge, deferring indefinitely a military service which was abolished by the time I had finished my prolonged, and no doubt indispensable, studies into the symbolism of the celestial rose in Dante's *Paradiso*.

I was envious of his good looks. His hair, fair and wavy, shadowed his pale forehead, and he bore an air of slightly dazed – and extremely fetching – vulnerability. My school friends found him fascinating, and were often drawn to his silent beauty in ways they could not even explain satisfactorily to themselves. He exercised a mysterious capacity to attract people to him which I certainly did not possess. This irritated me, since it suggested my publicly declared superiority might be undercut by attributes I lacked. If he coveted what came to me so easily, and which were an earnest of my merit, I was bitterly resentful of an appearance which he had done nothing to deserve. It was, of course, foolishness to be jealous of my brother's modest charm; a great deal of it lay in its artless absence of self-consciousness, and it was of little use to him, for he failed to employ it in the knowing way I would have done, had I been so favoured.

My own good fortune was not without its drawbacks. I found life at the Grammar School frightening, and in the early years I stayed away as much as I could, even writing notes to the Headmaster from our absent father, excusing my frequent truancies. One teacher, a lay preacher, to whom was entrusted such modest pas-

The Uses Of Adversity

toral care of the pupils as that dismal academy afforded, visited our house to look into the reasons for my poor attendance record at school. His errand was somewhat subverted by the presence of my brother; on seeing him, the teacher turned to me and said 'Why didn't you tell me you had such a lovely brother?' and playfully let his hand roam over his thigh. I was outraged by his thoughtless question. I was, after all, the object of his (unheard of) visit, and the interrogative struck me as an accusation, as though I had wilfully concealed the existence of my brother from those who would have been only too delighted to learn of it. Far from eliciting the cause of my loathing of school, I hardened myself against this insensitive man with his wheedling tone and wandering hands, and resolved never to disclose to him anything of what I thought or felt; even if he had exhibited the faintest interest in me, which he did not.

On rare occasions my brother and I went out together. I can recall one day in the summer holidays, when we walked my aunt's dog through the fields on a thundery afternoon, as huge anvil clouds blotted the sun and rain began to fall, scenting with caramel the burned grasses. Nothing happened on that memorable day; only I caught a glimpse of the companionship we might have enjoyed and the confidences we could have shared; a day saturated with rain and regret.

Later – I even remember the date, 1st August 1958 – we went to the theatre in London. This was just before he was to report for military service. It was a performance of an Australian play called *The Summer of the Seventeenth Doll*, about a group of friends who met each year to affirm their friendships and marriages; but in that seventeenth anniversary, everything fell apart and they quarrelled irrevocably. My brother was enchanted by the excursion. Afterwards, we went to eat in a dismal single-storey fish restaurant in Tottenham Court Road, where, after reading the menu, he asked for 'steak and chips.' I corrected him. He means 'skate and chips', I explained to the waiter, as though I were the child of an immigrant, interpreting for a parent who had failed to master the language.

Only one shared endeavour might have brought us closer. We always spent Christmas with Aunt May, my mother's only true friend and the only one of her sisters in whom she placed complete trust. The end of 1962 was shadowed by Aunt May's anxiety, since she had a hospital appointment in the new year She had become pale and exhausted, and she bruised easily – a slight pressure on the hand would bring put purple and yellow stains. She was diagnosed with leukaemia. We were shocked and distressed, since she had always been close to us. Her bed was brought downstairs into the middle room of the house, but this was a dingy chamber, in need of decoration. Jack and I offered to paint and paper the room. We did it together in a warm yellow, and within a couple of days it was ready. We worked energetically, but without speaking much, pre-occupied with the news that she would almost certainly not survive into the summer. Within a couple of weeks, unable to go upstairs, she retired to this chamber, and died in mid-July. On her last day, the doctor came, and fixing him with her fearless gaze, she said 'This is death, isn't it?' The doctor, recognising her strength, con-firmed it, and within a few hours she did die. Like our mother, she did not like evasion or euphemism. Even the shared act of devotion to our aunt failed to have any lasting effect upon my brother and me; and we kept our grief to ourselves.

When he finished his military service, my brother worked in the construction industry, helping to re-shape the face of our town, transforming its Gothic blood-red brick into geometric structures of concrete and glass. He worked as assistant supervisor on the building of the first multi-storey car park – a dazzling symbol of modernity and evidence that our town had indeed entered the 20th century – (a little late since it was already 1966). At that time, I was lamenting the passing of streets which were being torn down with such exuberance. This created yet another curious division between us. While he looked to an age of concrete and mobility, I was or-

The Uses Of Adversity

ganising protests against the construction of an Expressway, which would demolish almost a thousand houses, the 'little palaces' which people called the terraced houses which they had bought, improved and tended with such careful pride.

He was also called up by marriage. His marriage was arranged; not in the way that Jewish matchmakers or extended families in India organise them, but through the more or less inevitable acceptance of people that this was the natural order of things, that they were made for each other, the silent handsome man and the homely, affectionate young woman who wrote to him every day while he was in Germany. Her parents had worked in the boot and shoe industry. They were good Labour people, honest and hardworking; what could go wrong? He went into his marriage as passively as Glad had entered hers; and it seemed not to occur to her that it might be doomed to a similar swift decline.

It proved a sad error. The innocence of the protagonists and the eagerness of the families combined to create a marriage, which only re-awakened the dissatisfactions and the deep inner misery that childhood and adolescence had deposited in his trusting, receptive soul. He spoke, in a rare confessional moment, of having been buried alive.

He went to work in Zambia, partly in flight from the suffocating ties of kinship, both inherited and those apparently freely chosen. His work was concerned with the 'modernisation' of Lusaka, as it had previously been with the re-making of Northampton. The escape he had planned left him more isolated than ever; and after a year, he sent for his wife to join him. Between this invitation and her arrival, he had already met the woman who was to become his second wife. Only with her was he was able to discover himself; he flourished and defined an identity quite different from the submissive wraith he had been. He was already over thirty. His second marriage was a re-birth. This unhappily meant the death of his former self, the inauthentic shell made up of duty, self-effacement and obedience. He detached himself from everything and everyone in what now appeared an anterior existence. Even his name changed. He had always been 'Jack' or 'Jacky' to us. After his second marriage, no one called him anything but 'John'.

He literally re-made himself and in the process, discarded his birth family. The rift, which had run through our childhood, reinforced under the stringent laws of our mother's emotional apartheid, became final. There were a few clumsy gestures of reconciliation, an occasional meeting where the anger and resentment occasionally broke surface, and the parting was always acrimonious. The estrangement grew, until it became clear that only death would dissolve it.

After I had seen him for the last time at our mother's funeral, I grieved for him. I woke in the night, unable to believe what our sombre and unsparing childhood, that fretful visitation heavy with gloomy concealment, had done to us. The shock of his terminal farewell was even more wounding than the ritual leavetaking of our mother, which I had learned to expect from early infancy.

As the years passed, I thought less about my brother; but I was left with a dull ache, a sense of absence. All my close adult relationships have sought to fill that space. This took the form, not of seeking companions who resembled my brother – I didn't know him – but those who, I thought, resembled myself. I was seeking an identical twin, since the fraternal twin had been such a disappointment, and I wanted that relationship, not to complement, but to complete me.

When I learned that he had died, it was like confirmation of the body of a missing person had been found after a long search. He had vanished fifteen years earlier, and the remains, washed up on the shore of the long period that divided us, were identified as his.

There was another bitter irony in his death. He died of mesothelioma, an asbestos-related cancer. This was a consequence of his building work, which had produced multi-storey car-parks and concrete office blocks in our town, as well as in Lusaka and Windhoek in Namibia, where he also worked. These futuristic structures had been supplied with the miracle substance that was to make them proof against fire. He had no such protection, and his early working-class occupation determined his premature death. Although he had seemed in the 1960s to be an emissary of the time to come, altering the aspect of Victorian and colonial towns and cities, the past was not ready to release him; just as it held me in a different way.

As we grew older, what had appeared to be the class destination of our early years was transformed. The separation ceased to be so clearly based on social class, and mutated, so that it later came to appear that the distance between us was culturally rather than class-influenced. Dedicated to his family and his work, he was prosperous and at peace in the life he had made in a converted parsonage in the west of England. I had fulfilled my mother's ambition and had become a writer, an occupation which my brother held in the greatest contempt. Our mother didn't despise the work, but it never pleased her that I wrote principally about poor people. Nobody, she predicted – quite correctly – wanted to know about that. Had she not sacrificed herself, so that we should be protected from the humiliations of being poor? Why would I return to such things, if not out of a perverse desire to mock her efforts on our behalf? Nothing would come of it. She prided herself on her capacity for prophecy, and although many of her forecasts were conspicuously faulty, in this she was far from mistaken.

Joe, the man we did not know as our father, also contributed to the differences between us – a practical demonstration of the power of heredity, since neither of us had the faintest idea of his role in our lives until our mother's belated disclosure. He had been a highly skilled craftsman and builder, and my brother inherited his ability to mend and make beautiful things; he also worked on the restoration of many historic structures belonging to the Duchy of

Cornwall. Joe had also been a vehement Leftist, a member for some years of the Communist Party, as some of the books left with my mother testified. From him I received a hatred of orthodoxy, an instinctive dissent from all revealed ideologies and received wisdom; a revulsion which has proved a distinct handicap.

These secrets cast long, distorting shadows. By the time they were revealed to us, they had already lost their power. The old sensibility had decayed and secrecy itself seemed to have become superfluous. Indeed, so great has been the reversal, that we now suffer, not from a surfeit of concealment, but from its opposite – too many confessions. The extent of the road travelled can be seen in the necessity for silence on so many aspects of provincial society, to a complete absence of reticence in a world become metropolitan and global. Nothing is now too shaming or disgraceful to be told; and there is no holding back in the casual disclosure of elements of life which people, in that dour, simple time, would rather have died than disclose.

IX

Our mother had suffered severe post-natal depression. She had one day climbed onto the flat roof of the shop with the intention of jumping from the parapet with us in her arms. We were told this story early in our lives; perhaps to ensure that we should make no mistake about our redemptive purpose. It was, she gave us to understand, only for our sake that she had drawn back from suicide. It was our mission to prove to her this had been the right decision; although it is no easy thing for people to play the role of rescuer, particularly when they are infants, and the threat from which they are to deliver the one saved is only identified by mystifying allusion.

It appeared to me a great pity to have had two fathers, and to

The Uses Of Adversity

have known neither of them; rather wasteful really, especially in view of my own fragile sense of male identity. I grew up to see Sid as one who existed at a great distance, his emotional remoteness as powerful as the physical; so that to be male always appeared far off and unobtainable; to be aspired to perhaps, but not reached. Sid's prohibited body was desirable, hard and strong. Knowing nothing of the source of the taboo on him, I loved to be close to him, from where I could inhale the disturbing odour of outlawed sexuality. Sid's things always lay neglected on the floor of his room, while on cold mornings, his breath would have condensed on the widow-pane in icy blossoms that seemed to have sprung from his forbidden masculinity. I came to associate men with neglect, uncultivated abandon; they were growth in a wild mysterious wood that I was not permitted to explore.

My mother worked, an endless penitential labour, which suggested that in some part of her, she imagined that it really had all been her fault, a conviction that, however often she declared she had right and justice on her side, she didn't really believe it. She still felt culpable, and was moved by a need to expiate, atone for her gender. My early memories are all associated with her relentless activity, washing, cooking, scrubbing, chopping meat, serving in the shop, yet somehow never taking her eyes off me and my brother; endless, wearying work which, we understood was all for us. But it wasn't a gift. One day, it would have to be repaid, not in monetary form, not even in reciprocating the care she had lavished on us; but in ways undisclosed, so that we would never know whether or not we had succeeded. We would justify her existence.

She had tethered Sid to her by a dependency that grew out of his shaming illness. Joe was attached to her by his childlessness, and his late discovery of a need for paternity. She gave Joe enough information to excite his curiosity, to involve him in our fate, but not so as to permit the development of any independent relationship. Sometimes, he would park his car on the road along which she took us for walks, looking for early violets in the hedgerows, gathering primroses or bluebells. Then he would stop, wind down the window, using the contrived encounter as an excuse to look at his children. These interviews were always brief, made to seem like chance, lest they come under the censorious scrutiny of the neighbourhood. She would walk on, leaving him to drive slowly alongside, so that he might gain a last glimpse of us.

There were consolations in her position. She felt strong, and showed it in the vigour with which she poured away the contents of Sid's bucket, and cut up the carcases of animals, as if these had been the bodies of those who had injured her. It was only with May that she sometimes let go, released her anger and disappointment; but she mourned before no one the lack of any recognised outlet for her energy and intelligence. She was, however, also admired on the estate. Her discretion earned her a reputation for wisdom; and her role as counsellor was acknowledged by those who confided in her. She later became a school governor, and although no one would ever have guessed, it was a Labour Party appointment. Even the people from the big detached houses on the main road sometimes complained to her, not only about the uppitiness of the working class and their problem in keeping servants, but also confided their dissatisfactions of their marriage, and their anxieties about children who had become wastrels. In fact, she gained a kind of honorary middle class membership. Nobody ever knew her real views or opinions, which were a mixture of what would have been considered outrageous radicalism and a yearning to belong. This latter expressed itself in a desire for her children to conform to all the proprieties she had flouted; neither of us was able to gratify her in that respect.

On the night of the Blitz over Coventry, we were taken up to the roof with the neighbours to watch the pyrotechnics. Sid, ever the master of ceremonies, was making a collection for the show, although he insisted it was for the war effort. 'See', Sid was saying,

The Uses Of Adversity

not without a subdued exultation, 'it'll be our turn next. Lord Haw-Haw said so on the wireless. He said 'Northampton, it's your turn tomorrow' People looked at him and wondered whose side he was on. 'Well', he said, 'he's done wonders for his country, I don't care what anybody says.' 'Shut up, Sid', his wife said, 'You don't know what you're saying. In any case', she added sharply, in a rare outburst of candour, 'if you were in Germany, you'd be one of the first in the bloody camps.' He said nothing more, and his sympathies sank into abeyance under his wife's scorn. In the end, she gained from him what she had sought, something too few women received from their men until they were dead: respect.

X

Some days when I went to see her in the home, she wanted to talk. She would begin a gentle, ruminative monologue, which it was sometimes difficult to hear, because her voice had become fainter as a result of her fallen rib-cage. She must have known that her words would not go unrecorded; although I have no means of assessing their literal truth. Over and again, she would wonder about her husband. 'What did I see in him?' Of course, spent sexual interest is always a powerful illuminator of the flaws of the former loved one; but, despite her plainness, he had been far from the only man to have shown an interest in her.

At sixteen, after her brief employment in brush-manufacturing, she worked in the office of a shoe factory. Each morning on her way to work a boy from the Grammar School passed her on his bicycle. She often noticed him, apparently pausing for breath or to adjust his cap, at the bottom of the street as she turned into the main road that led to her workplace. She was touched and amused that he always raised his cap to her, as if she were an adult. One day, blushing, he compliment her. She wondered what had drawn him to her. He said it was her look of refinement; which was to her a high complement. They discovered they shared an interest in poetry. He gave her a copy of the poems of Christina Rossetti, some of which she could quote for the rest of her life

'Does the road wind uphill all the way?'

'Yes, to the very end.'

'Will the journey take the livelong day?'

'From morn till night, my friend.'

Such meetings without sequel or fulfilment, were later haloed with possibilities that contrasted with her later discontent. Unspoiled, they taunted her with what might have been. Of this boy, she said 'His father was a schoolteacher. I knew nothing could come of it, because I could never even ask him home. They had a big house overlooking the park, and one day he asked me to tea. Nobody had ever done that before. I was very nervous. My frock had a darn in it and I wore boys' boots. They had a cakestand with three silver plates. I looked at this object, and it spoke to me of the social gulf between us. He was a lovely, sensitive boy. I never knew what happened to him till years later, when he came into the shop. I recognised him straight away. His family had come to live nearby. He looked at me and said ''Didn't you used to be Gladys Youl?' I said 'I used to be lots of things.'

Suddenly, in the middle of a sentence, she would break off, her face contorted with pain, and asked me to lift her, because the rubber ring on which she sat was chafing her coccyx; or she would want her feet shifted, or her hands unlocked. This immobility was the reverse of rest, the enforced stillness far from the tranquillity she had craved; these only threw into sharper relief the inner perturbation.

She wouldn't watch television towards the end of her life. What is there on that thing, she would say, that can tell me anything I don't know? Her own life became a source of ceaseless reflection

The Uses Of Adversity

and instruction to her. In her sad, introspective refusal to be entertained, as was thought proper to the aged and impotent, there was an affirmation of life. She asked 'Why do people want to be distracted all the time? Is it because they can't bear to think about themselves? Even when people come to see their relatives here, they've got one eye on the tv, as if they're going to miss out on the meaning of life if they don't pay attention.'

Formerly, when I reflected on my mother's invasion of the lives of those close to her, I used to feel angry. Since she died, I see it in a somewhat different light. When I consider the traits and qualities I share with her, I can see that such characteristics are strewn randomly through the generations. We are the recipients of this chance distribution of features; and they mock our jealous protection of them in the name of autonomy or individuality. Some of the boundaries we erect around ourselves are arbitrary and perhaps less vital than we imagine; and my mother's movement in and out of her lives of her sisters and her sons was, perhaps, not quite the trespass it appeared then; for our existence is more permeable than we care to believe, and we do not, perhaps, have so much to guard from the scrutiny of those we love. Limits might be more fluid without necessarily damaging the core of our being, or whatever it is we seek to preserve; although when she opened my letters, took possession of my feelings and ordered my emotions, it certainly didn't seem benign.

Jeremy Seabrook

PART FIVE

I

Secrets spoil with keeping. They become hard, encrusted with unshared memories. It must have taken a great effort for her not to speak to my brother and me of her life until we were in our mid-thirties. We knew there was something waiting to be told, from the mystery she had spun around everyday life for as long as we could remember. She would sigh and say 'You'll know one day.' 'What?' we would ask eagerly. 'Never you mind', she would reply. Sometimes it was 'You'll know when you haven't got me.' 'Why, where are you going?' 'In my bloody grave, that's where.' Sometimes she talked to herself 'Oh dear, mother, is it worth it?' a question we didn't dare to ask the meaning of. Between her and us lay the unspoken; and it gave off a bitter graveyard aroma that deterred and silenced us.

Just as she could not bring herself to disclose to us the stories she felt were too terrible to be told, I could not bear to acknowledge to her that I was gay, although I longed to do so. When I first went to Cambridge Uncle Arthur drove me there in his Ford Zephyr, I think it was. He stood in the middle of Trinity Great Court and looked round with an expert and appraising eye. He sniffed and said 'All these men cooped up together. It's a breeding ground for homerbloodysexuality.' (he made of it a word of nine syllables). 'Stands to reason.' He also believed that this was an affliction of the upper classes. Aunt May, his wife, shuddered, and said 'Please God may it never touch any of us.' This was scarcely a propitious atmosphere in which to make avowals; so I kept it to myself.

So severe were the unexplained taboos on sex, my own sexuality was frozen under her influence. Once, shortly after I returned from Cambridge, I answered an advertisement in the *New Statesman* placed by a man who claimed to be looking for a holiday companion. It was known that this was code for a sexual contact in a time before the decriminalisation of homosexuality. I had given up hope of receiving a reply when a letter came, offering me an appointment to meet at Knightsbridge Tube Station some two weeks hence. I told my mother I was going to the theatre, and she demanded to see the ticket. She repeated her belief in the certain mischief of anyone still out after 9.30 at night was either thieving or whore-hopping.' I assured her, not quite truthfully, that nothing was further from my mind.

I arrived at the tube station early, and eagerly scanned the faces of all lone males who emerged, as well as those who seemed to be waiting for someone. Patrick would be carrying a copy of the magazine which he assured me would be unlikely to lead to embarrassing errors in that quarter of London. I recognised him immediately. In his late twenties, he was dark and thickset, and had an accent I knew from Cambridge. I imagined that we would 'dine' somewhere, for such were my fantasies about how contacts like this would be followed up. Instead, he suggested we take a walk in Hyde Park. It was drizzling, and I was puzzled by what appeared an eccentric choice of entertainment. We walked away from the misty orange light of the street-lamps. The plane trees were bare and bore trembling silver buds. A chill breeze had driven everyone away from the unsheltered places. In the middle of a patch of darkness he ordered me peremptorily to show him my cock. Shocked and frightened, I fled.

She was still up when I got home, her hair in its night-time plait, the cup of bed-time hot milk steaming on the table; when she

The Uses Of Adversity

asked me how I enjoyed the theatre, I said 'It was all right.' 'What was it about?' 'You wouldn't understand', I said curtly and went upstairs.

It turned out that my flight, far from discouraging my friend, only strengthened his ardour. He wrote a letter which my mother intercepted. She was quite unaware of the existence of boundaries, and, like all her brothers and sisters, walked in and out of each other's lives as they entered and left each other's houses; without announcing themselves, without knocking. Their life was not as highly individualised as it was to become, but was a pooled or collective experience, in which they were custodians of each other's well-being, but also of their conduct.

I came home from the Library one day. Her body tense and clenched, she looked as if she had been crying. 'What's wrong?' My anxiety responded to hers. She maintained a silence that drew from me more urgent entreaties to tell me what was troubling her. 'What is it?' 'It's this', she cried dramatically, after a histrionic display of suffering, drawing from her apron a crumpled sheet of paper which she threw down on the table. 'It's a love letter. A love letter from a man to my son.' Then, raising her fury to a higher pitch she addressed me 'Is it men you want? Is that it? Is it men you want?' Weakly I protested 'No Mum, 'course not.' I showed her the apparently innocuous advertisement to which I had responded. She said 'It would kill me, you know that.' Even under stress I wanted to say that there was no known record of any death by disclosure of another's sexuality; but of course, I remained silent.

When her fury had ebbed, she looked at me with sorrowful grey eyes, pleading that all she wanted to do was protect me from harm. My pity for her only bound me closer.

II

In the summer of 1959, just before my final year at Cambridge, I went away from home for the first time. Officially, this was to further my study of Italian, for which I had been awarded a bursary by the Italian government, a piece of long-vanished official largesse, which would enable me to spend three months in Rome. More immediately, I thought it might give me an opportunity to investigate sexual possibilities beyond the reach of her influence, which was so intense that even Cambridge did not place me beyond the orbit of her sweeping knowingness.

I had come, I also told myself, to the land of Dante and Petrarch, to improve myself, culturally, intellectually and spiritually. But like my fellow-students, who were there with lighter purposes in mind – to get drunk, have fun and lose their virginity, primitive erotic adventures in an unliberated age – I secretly hoped *something would happen*. I knew that same-sex relationships were not criminal offences on the continent as they still were at home. I stayed in a gloomy pensione close to the Spanish Steps, and went daily to the classroom in a narrow street which trapped orange wedges of sunlight that turned the upper storeys of buildings into aerial palaces, another, more magical city that shimmered above the shadowed streets below.

Every day after class I installed myself on the steep slope of the balustrade at the top of the Spanish Steps, expecting much of a place that promised experiences unavailable in Northampton.

They were slow in coming. I looked searchingly into the eyes of passers-by. Too many of them had Northern English accents; women who walked in defensive groups, hugging their handbags to their bodies in anticipation of Italian pickpockets and cutpurses, against whom tour organisers had warned them to be on their guard.

The Uses Of Adversity

One afternoon, when the city was flooded with molten gold and the heat caused the buildings on the other side of the Piazza di Spagna to disintegrate, a slim young man materialised out of the fumes, and seated himself on the opposite side of the balustrade, in a posture unmistakeably symmetrical to my own. It was suffocatingly hot, desire and abandon in the air. My companion – for so I thought of him – smiled. His hair was bronze, his skin pale and eyes of such luminosity that they seemed to glow from within, like the candle in the hollow head of a pumpkin at Hallowe'en. He wore as striped matelot jersey and tight jeans, and I thought him the most beautiful creature I had ever seen.

He came over to me and offered me a cigarette. These were French, *Gitanes*, and they gave off a scent that lingered in hair and clothes, redolent of sexual adventure. I answered in Italian – the first useful conversation I had had in that melodious tongue, although he spoke with a coarse Roman accent. He asked me why I was alone, a question which seemed to me a thrilling preamble to relationship, the nature of which I had no difficulty in imagining. This was confirmed by his next question. Do you have a girl friend? No. He did, he said, but she only wanted money. I ought, perhaps, to have been on my guard at this, but I was under such an enchantment that I was all candour and conspicuous admiration. He asked me if I liked girls. I said yes, but that I also liked friendship with boys. He said would you like me to be your friend. Of course. *Dovresti pagare*, he said. It will cost you.

I understood the nature of his calling. He wanted a thousand lire and the bracelet I was wearing. This was a showy piece of kitsch I had exchanged with a young woman friend in Cambridge, an eternity love-bangle, and therefore to be bartered away at the first opportunity for dalliance. I had no difficulty in parting with it. A thousand lire, too, seemed a small price to pay for initiation into friendship with an Italian boy. Who, I reflected, must have been younger than I was, no more than seventeen or eighteen.

We walked in silence to the Villa Borghese. Dry leaves crunched like bone beneath our feet. We came to an alley bordered by dark flames of cypress trees, which smouldered in a hot resinous fragrance. He put two fingers to his mouth and produced a shrill whistle. Out of nowhere, a child of ten or eleven appeared. He told him to watch out for other walkers, and to be sure to give a signal if anyone approached. He then sat down, unzipped his fly and invited me to masturbate him.

This brief meeting was as close as I came to the amorous entanglements of my fellow-students. It was abridged by the sudden recollection that this was the afternoon of the examination for the diploma I would require in order to dislodge the bursary from its bureaucratic eyrie. I hastily offered the gifts demanded by the boy, and fled, so as not to miss my appointment with the examiner. In the rush, I failed to notice that as I sat on the grassy knoll, my shoe had rested in shit, human shit, richly dark and odorous.

The boy had promised to meet the following day, with a hint of more intimate relations; but naturally, after this disturbing encounter, I avoided both the Spanish Steps and the Villa Borghese. In any case, two days later, I returned to the *pensione* to discover the money and travellers' cheques, which I had negligently left on the table of my room, had vanished. I did not associate the robbery with the vision on the Spanish Steps, but I caught sight of the boy in the dim interior of the building. My trip was abruptly curtailed, and I left, arriving home in Northampton, not two long and experience-filled months later, as I had planned, but a paltry and shaming couple of weeks after my ceremonial departure.

III

As consolation for this disappointment – which pleased my mother mightily, for she had always remarked on my shiftlessness – she suggested we might take advantage of what was one of the warmest summers of the century, and spend a couple of weeks at the seaside. It would have been difficult to devise a less satisfactory form of recuperation. My mother and I, unaware of each other's secrets which impeded all communication between us, found in one another's company a loving irritant. We should have known better.

But it seemed a more manageable excursion that my outlandish jaunt to the continent, on which I maintained a – for my mother, inexplicable – reticence, although I admitted to carelessness in letting myself be robbed, and to folly in abridging my stay and forfeiting the bursary. Why had I not sought justice, gone to the police, complained to the authorities? I tried to explain that 'authorities' in Rome were unlike anything known in Northampton. I associated the guilt of my meeting with the boy with the loss of my belongings, and the last thing I wanted was for connections to be made where I suspected they might well have existed. Italy was, just then, coming into prominence as a tourist destination. It had previously been associated, in our provincial mind, with prisoners of war, who, in the 1940s, had passed the shop every day in crowded buses taking them to their place of labour, workers in the brickfields of Bedfordshire, small dark men from Calabria, with moustaches, muscles and skin reddened by the heat of the kilns. Italians as models of irresistible sexuality, vying with each other to seduce pallid English signorinas (or even young English men in search of initiation) were still only a faint rumour of what they were to become.

It was decided we would go Paignton in Devon. For my mother, already suffering mildly from the agoraphobia that would later imprison her indoors – this was a major upheaval. Packing was a labour of Sisyphus: no sooner had every last thing been packed, than it all had to be taken out again to make sure that some trivial item had not been omitted. The departure itself was a scarcely tolerable burden. How many times the gas-taps had to be tested to make sure they were in the off position, with what effort the water pipe had to be closed so that the pipes should not freeze in an August heatwave; how discreetly the note to the milkman not to deliver had to be concealed beneath the bottle on the step. For my mother, every leave-taking, the briefest departure from home always foreshadowed something more final; an aspect of life which has also been part of her onerous bequest to me.

She had booked us into a boarding house recommended by a neighbour – clean, wholesome fare at reasonable prices. We carried our luggage like refugees; 'crossing London' at that time having, to people from the country, something of the epic properties of crossing the Alps. We asked directions several times, but only of the most inoffensive-looking people, because everyone knew London was full of thieves and vagabonds, and we wore our provincial status, not in our clothing, but in the perspiring anxiety of our faces and the mystified gaze we turned upon conflicting signs and notices. The trouble with begging instruction of the harmless was that these often turned out to be, either strangers like ourselves, or of infirm understanding, so that little reliance could be placed on the information they gave.

The train from Paddington was hot and crowded, since holidays still retained awkward associations with wartime evacuation: luggage piled high in the corridors, while some people still conveyed their possessions by trunk, padlocked metal caskets, which railway personnel accepted as part of their duty to carry to and from the train.

We walked to our boarding house, about ten minutes from the station, in an Edwardian avenue of detached houses, most of them transformed into holiday hotels with names from elsewhere –

The Uses Of Adversity

Braemar, Capri, Trouville or St Brelade's; hanging baskets of geraniums, pebble dashed walls, hydrangeas and crazy paving welcomed us to the particular site of hospitality we had chosen. Inside, it was spotless, but with the fussy paraphernalia of an already antique form of homeliness – pink velvet curtains, rosy wallpaper, warming pans, Toby jugs and pictures of pussy-cats and Mabel Lucie Atwell children on the walls. The motif of the carpets suggested whirlpools of blood, while boughs of plastic lilacs gushed from what looked like funerary urns.

We were just in time for the evening meal, a sparing feast, although the napery and cutlery gleamed, and late sunshine through the laburnums superimposed another pattern on the rose-bower wall. Five guineas a week bought an impeccable gentility, suppressed coughs and talk vanishingly small from the mostly elderly guests. My mother and I sat in constrained silence, waiting for our poached egg on toast garnished with a round of tomato. I think we both knew immediately that this expedition was a terrible mistake. We spoke to each other with excruciating politeness, and exchanged details of our provenance with fellow-boarders – a major and his lady who had recently returned from Cyrenaica in Libya, where, we learned there was a British military base; an elderly couple from Chorley, which sounded like a jolly place, although if it was, it had communicated to these representatives of it no trace of gaiety, and a lady and her companion – for so they announced themselves – who had come down from Cheltenham. They spoke as though they had travelled from a distant climatic zone to enjoy the healing fraicheurs of Devon.

Out of a context in which we had each learned to accommodate our secrets, my mother and I were paralysed by enforced public proximity. She had wanted, at that time, to tell me her story, but she had held back, not wanting, she said 'to spoil a holiday', which was certainly no festival. She also perhaps didn't want to disturb something she referred to as 'my studies', always in the plural; my pedagogic wanderings with Dante and Proust. It didn't even occur to me to make any disclosures, the unspeakable aberration that was my sexuality, outlawed at that time and object of a prohibition almost as dreadful as that which surrounded the sibilant menace of her husband's disease.

How could such an outing have been anything but calamity? I remember the choking ennui of the unspoken, The sun-bleached streets of Paignton, somnolent and deserted in the long afternoons of late August, only reflected the emptiness of the hours to be got through, each one an obstacle. We were both living elsewhere, ironically, with remote male companions, she in her guilt-stained past, pondering on the errant man's needs she had been unable (unworthy?) to fulfil, and I in a distant future, where I would surely have met the man who was to transform my life.

IV

I might have met him in Paignton. I went for long walks on my own. Actually, these were not walks, but voyages of exploration, a one-person search party for a missing self. I looked full into the face of every male between the ages of about eighteen and forty, a mute interrogation as to whether he were the one destined to relieve me of this unique sense of oppressive strangeness. Since I had never disclosed to anyone the shaming fact of what I understood was my deviancy, I had no way of knowing that it was far less particular than I imagined. I later found out that as many as eight or ten of my peers in the VI Form were gay; but in that time of straitened provincial tension, we never got round to admitting it to one another, even though we were constant companions, united in a sensibility we could neither define nor admit to. I later wondered whether there were not some obscure social determinant in this

The Uses Of Adversity

apparent coincidence; perhaps something about the weakening of industrial disciplines which had, until a generation offered alternatives to the dominance of manual labour, suppressed at source such things?

Such speculation was for the future. Off I went, round the flowerbeds, the orange-and-lemon marigolds and silvery artemesia, purple petunias and ubiquitous geraniums, along the cliff with my copy of the Complete Dante bound in red. I walked so far I sank, exhausted, onto the grass looking out at the sea, which I detested for its repetitiveness: the waves that broke pointlessly on the sand, and then sucked the bladderwrack and ice-cream papers into the mouth of the ocean; the clash of pebbles stirred by the retreating waves; the sun striking live fluid sparks from the water; everything irritated me, but nothing more than the slow passage of the hours between insipid meals that punctuated the time in that genteel cage of our shared penitential holiday.

One day, I went out early and occupied a small green promontory on the cliff. It was a clear morning, with only the sound of the gulls on the wind. I felt a melancholy relief that my mother had fallen in with the military man and his wife. I could only imagine that the torpor of the resort, the last resort, had brought them together. Later, when I joined them, I was surprised to discover they had spent the day discussing religion, and found themselves united by a common unbelief.

My solitude on the knoll was disturbed by the arrival of a stranger, who calmly sat down beside me on the little piece of land at the cliff's edge. He said nothing, but after a few minutes began to undress. He folded his clothes neatly beside him, until he had stripped down to a pair of red swimming trunks. He then lay down in the sun and closed his eyes. He was about twenty seven, with tattoos on both arms. One said Mother, and on the other was a tombstone in red and blue. In place of the name of the occupant of the grave was written in blue ink R.I.P. LOVE.

There was no one near us. Why had he chosen this particular spot? Had I usurped his customary place, and was he willing me to depart? Diligently, I opened my Dante and pretended to concentrate on some particularly impenetrable verses of Purgatorio. My eyes kept stealing from the page to the body that was scarcely a foot from where I sat, smooth, slightly sunburnt skin, fair body-hair iridescent as the breeze moved it in the sun. He laced his hands behind his head, and the ellipse of his muscles contracted, and I could smell the musky odour from the tangle of hair in the armpit. I glanced at the red tumulus of his genitals, which from time to time, he stroked tenderly. I assumed he was as unaware of my presence as I was conscious of his. From the vulnerable whorl of the navel, a herringbone of hair darted to the edge of his trunks, which were taut over the hips, so that a slight aperture of dark shadow stood between the tight fabric and the lean protuberance of bone. Disturbed but transfixed, I could neither address him nor leave. He had such an air of containment I could not believe he noticed me at all. What enviable confidence in his right to exist in youthful splendour, lying with such naked negligence on the dry salty grass – I could not have imagined any such public abandon, nor any display of my body, which, if I had ever exposed it to sun and wind, I had certainly not done so with the pride and assurance that he showed.

I could not think that, in spite of the considerable space around us, he should have chosen to lie so close to me, a taunt and an empty temptation, since I did not dare to speak. I did not move and neither did he. The sun inscribed its burning arc on the sky, sank towards the sea, an orange marigold on a silver stalk; and still I waited, thinking he might begin some trivial conversation, although I also knew the moment to initiate communication was long past. He familiar he became in the few hours we had remained in the same place, I not reading Dante, he feigning sleep, although I am sure he was conscious all the time; but I told myself he had come solely for the sun, to deepen the red-brown glow of his skin,

The Uses Of Adversity

the faint flaking of his scorched face.

I waited for him to go, which he did just before dark. He rose, stretched, all the while displaying his straight thorax and the corrugation of his rib-cage, the shifting mound of his sex, the cascade of hair that fell over his face as he stood up. He stepped into his trousers, tugged the short-sleeved green shirt over his head, slipped his feet into sandals he had not even unbuckled, and disappeared down the slope towards the road, without acknowledgement or even a glance.

How bereft I felt when he had gone, a premonition of loss of something I had never possessed. I remained a few minutes. The breeze was cool and the indigo water retained a faint stain of daylight that had almost vanished from the sky. How savourless everything seemed afterwards, the prospect of thinly-spread bread and butter cut into triangles, the rock cakes with their hard black currants, weak tea and a slice of pink meat. And my mother would be worried to death about what had become of me, and I would be unable to tell her, because the nothing she had predicted had indeed become of me.

He didn't return to the spot, although I did, the next day, and the one after that. Only five days of the holiday had elapsed. Even my mother, accustomed to my silences and withdrawals, noticed that I was more despondent than ever. I resented her, because I thought it was she who had endowed me with such meagre attractions that, if I wanted anything, I would have to pay for it; there would have to be compensation for anyone who bestowed his company upon me. This was followed by remorse; and only much later by a realisation that it was not especially my qualities that were wanting, but her low evaluation of them, which was not her true assessment, but which she had employed as a strategy to prevent me from straying. The trouble was that I had absorbed this falsely miserable estimate, and lived up (or down) to it.

In the following two days, I wrote an essay on Dante, a copy of which remains with me after all these years. Since, of all the callow productivity of my years at university, this alone is associated with the mood of that eventful but unfulfilling summer. My aunt had recently given me a typewriter, a scratchy metal portable, with a ribbon half-black, half-red, which jumped each time a kept was struck so the text appeared in two colours on the page. It was about the love that exists in the heart of the lover before he ever gazes upon her who will release it in him. Prompted by own solitary exaltations, I had had my own glimpse of a profane beatific vision.

At the end of the first week my mother looked at me and said 'Do you want to go home?' I could have wept with relief. We departed on the Monday, alleging sickness in the family – a truth which we imagined to be falsehood. To follow our separate paths was a burden lifted: we could not wait to be alone with the heavy secrets that had lain between us like lead while we were away from home.

I never again went away with my mother, although she did come to stay with me and my partner from time to time many years later. I never came out to her as gay. There was no need to do so, since she simply accepted my relationship with him, without question or wonder; and it was he who was with her when she died.

V

My mother's lifelong sickness was an outcrop of a deeper ill-being. She had never been at home in life. She suffered a level of estrangement from existence itself that cannot be ascribed simply to belonging to one society or another. She and I both knew this, but this did not mean that our apprehension of the follies and cruelties of the society we did inhabit were false. On the contrary; it sharpened our sense of what was amenable to social improvement and

The Uses Of Adversity

what was irremediable. We both saw the absurdity of social arrangements which had begun to promise people freedom from the necessary afflictions of being – escape from ageing, sickness and loss – and which professed its powerlessness to do anything very much to ease alterable afflictions like poverty and distress.

If I studied her attentively in her later years, this was because of what such observation could teach me about myself and the sombre heritage we shared. When she placed her hand over her face, this was a screen to shield her from a world from which she was already exiled. She would close her eyes, and I understood her flight from the landscaped environment, in which everything had been prepared for a serene evening of life, into which her desperately turbulent old age had been transplanted.

I sat with her in this withdrawn state, rising now and again to adjust the cushion against the pink of her scalp visible through the thinning grey hair, to allow her to drink from the plastic cup with its spill-proof lip, to lift her for a few moments as a relief from a posture she could not control. I thought of the insistent demands I had once made on her, to which she had responded every time; but there was nothing I could do in the brief hours we spent together. I could not give her the comfort she had offered me, tell her that everything would be all right, that things would soon be better, that the sandman would come, and she could have the moon and stars to play with if she didn't cry. She had not failed me, as I was bound to fail her, despite the symmetry of my dependency then and hers now.

I could anticipate all her feelings, apprehend her experience. My mother had always wanted company in her desolation. She need not have made such efforts to secure it, for she already had it; yet even my involuntary inherited companionship could not console her, any more than it brought me any satisfaction.

Jeremy Seabrook

VI

She reverted all the time to her childhood; and she saw continuities between life in the shabby brown-painted terraced houses of her early life. Then, they had had orange-boxes for furniture, sacks at the window for curtains, bare floorboards and only a length of scuffed lino. The décor of the nursing home could not have been more different. with its tepid, hushed corridors and double glazing, its chintzy covers and winged chairs looking out onto the cunningly contrived contours of the golf course. 'How is it the same then?' 'They made money out of us when we had nothing, and they're taking it away from us now. Only the setting is different. From rags and poverty to a padded cell. No wonder they treat us as if we'd lost our senses; they think we won't notice.'

She looked back in wonder, at a family that had grown, wild and plentiful as summer weeds, but had been scattered by time and change, its place taken by an expensive solitude, and an unaccountable inability to care for those we love; a mysterious mixture of liberation and impotence, of self-cancelling emancipations. My mother and aunt joined the sixty or seventy old people in the nursing-home who had become the object of other people's labour. Most of the staff were young women, some tender young girls who could not bear the contact with old age, querulousness and incontinence; some left in tears, unable to complete their first day's work. Others resented the inadequate pay for difficult work and punished the old people for it; the young looked at the elderly across the gap of time, as if they were peering for the first time into another culture, as, indeed, many of them were. There were others, middle-aged women, imaginative, compassionate people, who saw themselves and their own loved ones in the blanched faces and withered skin, and who, tender and solicitous, did their best to hearten those in their charge. Yet others, temporary agency workers, came and went by the day, knew nothing of the routine; some slept in the small hours in defiance of the terms of their contract, and failed to hear the cries for the commode or for a helpless body to be turned, trapped by arthritic rigors and wasted muscles.

The nursing home had been an investment by a company that had envisaged this beautifully tended site as a place for the well-to-do elderly. It was to have been a refuge, where sweet old ladies out of Cranford would take tea in bone-china cups and read their library books, until one day they would quietly set aside their needlework, yield a sigh and *pass away* rather than die, with dignity, their affairs in order. This proved illusion. Even those who had apparently limitless money became confused or incontinent, angry, undermined by dementia. They howled with rage and pain, wept for lost family, relatives who failed to appear, friends who had died before them. The home had to take more and more people supported by the State, and the idea of genteel twilight was overtaken by the miseries of dark night.

VII

Glad often said she had lived too long, but she didn't want to die. She wanted someone to rescue her. Bring me back, was her silent order to me, from this decline. If you cannot hold me back from death, a least come with me.

I had mourned her in advance. I had worked so hard at the grief I had imagined from my earliest childhood. Anticipating her loss had been a preoccupation for as long as I could remember. If I was able clearly to monitor every stage in her deterioration, this was because I had already lived through it beforehand, and expended so much anxiety in presentiment. I had foreseen every conceivable death: the shrunken body and the noiseless gnawing of the cancer within, the sudden accident, the heart attack, the face contorted by a stroke. Whenever I was at home in Northampton, I often got up in the night to listen for the sound of her breathing. I sometimes even opened the door to watch for the rise and fall of the candle-wick bedspread as it responded to the rhythm of her sleeping body. It was as though I could not bear to be taken by surprise by death or loss, but had to be constantly watchful for their approach. I sought to pay back the guilt, by instalments, as it were, before she died, in order not to be convulsed by her death.

Of course I would not go with her, even though I had accompanied her into some of the remote places where she had lived, the god-forsaken retreats to which her sensibility had banished her. I sat with her long days while Aunt Em was in her final stay in hospital. And in the hours of occupationless intimacy, all the other people she had been came back: the young mother with the wavering short-lived gaiety, who applied lipstick only on Tuesdays before her appointments with Joe; for we were affected by her light-heartedness as we skipped along beside her as she promised she would bring us, luxury of luxuries, a Bakewell tart for tea. She returned in other guises too, the powerful moral presence that hovered over our wrongdoings, which *would be the death of her*, if we didn't do as bade us; the compassionate listener in the shop, as the women of the estate bared their sorrows, a nakedness more shocking than any physical state of undress; the voracious reader of the books I brought home from school and university, to which she brought her own judgments, saying Madame Bovary was not a good book because Emma was such a shallow, flighty woman. She told me that, as an adolescent, she had haunted the Public Library and looked hungrily at names on the spines of books, and had wondered what kind of a woman Go-Ethe could be. There was, too, among the personages we had known, the spurned wife, the instrumental adulterer, the keeper of secrets and finally, the woman who told us her story only when both men were dead, and we could not go to them for corroboration or denial.

It is hard for me to say now how much, or indeed, whether, I loved her. I was certainly both receptacle for her pain, and replica of her troubled personality. I knew also that it had always been my brother's healing acknowledgement of her suffering that she most desired. My brother would not been drawn into her distress. He appeared self-possessed and hence, unreachable; and he felt her attentions as an assault upon who he was; that was why he abandoned her to noisy remorse and bewilderment. She never knew exactly how she had wounded him, and he was never able to overcome it sufficiently to be able to reach out in reconciliation. Indeed, unreconciled describes her in every sense.

VIII

Although she was by now in her mid-eighties, people in the nursing-home still told her their secrets. Perhaps she gave off some scent of a retentive power. She was still in full possession of her mental faculties, a condition rare enough in the nursing-home to earn the respect of the staff and the dependency of some of the most vulnerable residents. The whispered confidences that had taken place over the shop counter were repeated in the winged armchairs. One woman told her she had been abandoned by her mother when she was ten months old. Her father died, and her three sisters placed in an orphanage. She was too young to be taken into an institution, so her mother, who went into domestic service, consigned her to a friend, who had five children of her own. Although never formally adopted, she was brought up as one of the family. As she grew up, she formed a deep attachment to one of the sons of the family. Her foster-mother suggested they should get married. 'Nobody knew I wasn't his real sister. They never legally adopted me, no papers, nothing. So I became famous for marrying my brother. It caused a lot of heartache because nobody knew we were not related, and we had grown up together. There were poison pen letters. The vicar came and told my mother it was sinful. My foster-mother tried to contact my birth mother, but she had vanished. Then she went to Somerset House to find my birth certificate. She couldn't find it, so she took someone else's, a stranger the same age as me.'

One of the few men in the home told her that his father had been a very strict disciplinarian. He had been in the army, and never in his life had he touched his son, neither in anger nor affection. His control of the family had been absolute, but he had been aloof and remote. He had never held him, cuddled him or demonstrated the slightest sign of affection. He told my mother that only after his father died, and he was looking at him in his coffin, he wondered if he might kiss him good-bye. He was by this time in his thirties. He bent down and kissed the waxen face. He told my mother he felt it had been a violation.

The subdued murmurings of these stories were the only movement in the still afternoon; they stirred the curtains, lingered around the dusty cornices, hung in the warm air. My mother had only to listen to people for them to tell her how wonderfully she understood them; even though she had not spoken a word.

It must have been bewildering for her, since she observed how secrets change over time; what had been matters for shame and concealment later became items of casual gossip. As antibiotics became widely available, sexually transmitted diseases were easily treatable; and she once heard somebody say that he would rather have a does of syph than the common cold, because at least it could be cured. She was angry and appalled by what seemed to her a degradation of her dignified silence of so many years. Her life had been poisoned by her secret knowledge that she had been unable to measure against the equally dumb knowing of others who had also

The Uses Of Adversity

carried a lifetime's secrets *to the grave*, as they sometimes solemnly said. She was disoriented by social change that seemed to make light of an affliction that had been as shocking as HIV and AIDS were to become in the 1980s.

She noted also that, far from maintaining a discreet reticence as the twentieth century drew towards its close, people could not wait to tell the world everything. There is, she said, nothing too terrible to be told: no disgrace, no dishonour so unspeakable it cannot be told. The air was suddenly thick with people recounting their lives incontinently, often to the empty air. They cannot tell their tale quickly enough, since nobody is really listening. She found it impossible to accept that *none of it really mattered.*

Perhaps that was why she asked me not to write about her when she was dead. Since I had already done so while she lived, it was a prohibition bound to be broken; my obedience to her had its limits; so that even what is intended as a tribute to her is also a betrayal; part of an inextricable tangle of love, dependency, loss, resentment and admiration for her tenacity and endurance.

IX

When our mother finally revealed to my brother and me everything that had happened we were neither shocked, nor particularly upset. On the contrary – what had been obscure and opaque suddenly became explicable. Oh, that was why you said this or did that, or forbade this or recommended something else. Even so, some aspects of her morality remained inexplicable. She would sometimes hold up the third finger of her left hand, where the gold band was diminished by the swollen flesh that surrounded it and said 'There's no happiness outside of the wedding ring.' How she had salvaged that particular piece of wisdom from her savage experience it is difficult to say. I could only assume hat she was referring to the hopes she may have placed in Joe, hopes to which she had never admitted, but which might have been cruelly disappointed. Or perhaps she meant the sexual divagations of Sid. But is was an incongruous admonition, both to me and my brother, in the light of the injuries of its closed circle.

She was seventy when she made her disclosure, and we were in our mid thirties. She recounted the story with great solemnity and ceremony, as she had always intended to do. In keeping with the apartness of our lives, she told each of us separately; and in a rare example of convergence of our feelings, our reaction was identical. Neither of us felt it anything of a privation, that Sid should be divested of a paternity for which he had shown so little aptitude.

On her seventieth birthday, my partner and I went to spend two days with her and my aunt. It was a resplendent weekend in June. The pale porcelain cups of dog-roses lay scattered across the hedgerows, the fields were bright with ox-eye daisies and poppies among high purple grasses. The sun poured from a cloudless sky, and my mother wore a blouse I had brought for her from Paris so many years before that it was faded and unfashionable; but she retained it for its hint of foreign sophistication and the fact that it had been one of the few personal gifts I had ever offered her.

She had made up her mind that we should take her out to lunch on both days. On Saturday, we went to Olney, where Sid had been raised; and on Sunday to Towcester, close to Joe's village; symbolic if valedictory visits that would at last bring together the two men, united in death as they had been separated in life.

On the Saturday afternoon, we strolled along Olney High Street, with its superior antique shops, where early nineteenth century grandfather clocks and Chinese vases were on display; newsagents windows advertising for reliable domestic help and offering for sale a Cortina only one year old; market stalls where only the old season's carrots, parsnips and greens were piled on rough trestles. We came to the memorial bench to Sid's father, which had been disfigured by lichen and graffiti. We looked at the long-closed slaughterhouse; the pentagonal house-building was still a butcher's shop, only slightly altered from the days when its dark interior had attracted us, and ice-cold water was drawn into the shallow plaster sink by a pump from a well in the garden. The garden path was still tessellated with beige and blue Victorian tiles, and on the fuschia bushes still danced the purple and scarlet ballerinas. We then drove through the neighbouring villages, names evocative of vanished summers – Newton Blossomville, Yardley Hastings and Emberton. Glad was silent, and we linked arms, the two sisters with me and my partner, an enigmatic family group, forerunner of new patterns of elective kinship and familial structure, since we would spend much time together in the seventeen years she was yet to live.

The following day, we had lunch in a converted barn on the dusty A5; and paused at the rambling sandstone cottage where Joe had lived. It now had green shutters, but the garden was well-tended, red tulips collapsed under the weight of their dying blossom, the already dying tapers of lilac and roses which had all burst into spontaneous bloom that weekend. The air of the countryside was thick with the acrid pollen of cream elderflowers and the flat planes of cow-parsley, their pale blossoms extinguished by rapeseed, its violent yellow flowers alien in the soft tones of the English countryside.

On the Sunday afternoon, she said 'I've got something to tell you.' Although she had anticipated this moment for thirty five years – and delayed it constantly, because she cannot have believed that we would be traumatised by her revelations once we were adult – when it came, it was calm, matter-of-fact and distinctly un-dramatic. Why had she kept it to herself for so long? Perhaps silence had entered her soul, it had become part of who she was, her identity as woman-with-secret; and as time went by, she perhaps feared that, instead of being relieved of a great burden, she might feel voided of what had given her life content for so long. Her own restraint in the narrating of it was matched by the quiet approbation of her conduct which I expressed. I think she was disappointed by my response. Did she perhaps want me to cry out and to accuse her? Perhaps she had expected that I would be as overwhelmed as she had been; and although I had been, as it were, a major if involuntary protagonist in the story, experience is never transferable; so although I could readily understand the heroic forbearance she had exercised, my reaction was considered and contained. Thinking, perhaps, that what she had told me was too terrible for me to absorb in a single telling, she repeated it. 'Did I do the right thing?' she asked. I said to her 'It was the best day's work you ever did', and I thanked her for all she had done for us. I kissed her cheek. Even her tears tasted, not of salt, but of the corrosive acid of her bitterness.

She was not to know that this significant day in her life was to be equally so for me. My partner and I left the old ladies in the early evening. My aunt had made a Victoria sponge, which she had wrapped in tissue paper and place in a tin that had held Cadbury's Roses chocolates. We stopped the car at Yardley Gobion, a village not very far from Northampton. We sat on a grassy slope to watch the sun go down, and cut into the soft sponge cake with a knife Aunt Em had provided. I can picture the scene: behind us a grey wall against which a yellow rose was growing in profuse bloom. A light Westerly breeze scattered some of the lemon flakes of the roses onto where we sat; and I cried for my mother and aunt, and also for myself, since I realised that not until this moment was I able to retrieve my feelings held fast in the dark places where she had sequestered them, and offer them to what was my first – and only – significant relationship with an adult.

X

As soon as my mother had parted with her secret, she began to shake. Not the faint tremor that comes gradually with ageing, but an uncontrollable involuntary shiver; as though retention of the story had been the only thing holding her together. This had been at the root of her grim resolve not to yield. She had for so many years anticipated and longed for the future, but when it came, it detached her sons from her and added to the troubled desertions of her life. Once gone, the scars of secrecy haunted her in the form of elusive sicknesses which defied the professionals into whose care she passed. They duly prescribed all the drowsy remedies in their expanding pharmacopia, but could not touch the torn spirit.

She knew the shaking was a result of letting go. She was told she had Parkinson's disease. She said 'What do they know?' She felt a debility that came from the effort of containing what seemed like a thirty-five-year-long pregnancy; the removal of a cancer of the sentiments. It wasn't so much the horror of her secret that was revealed by the telling of it, as the function it had played in her life: it had provided the ballast that kept her stable.

During those years, she said, she had seen so much stripped away; the family broken and dispersed, the great reservoir of humanity in which she had grown, depleted and gone. The twelve children of her generation, whose lives had been so intertwined, boys and girls sleeping head to toe in their childhood, so as to avoid improper contact, themselves produced only twelve children between them; and these grew up to be virtual strangers to each other. A way of life had perished; and whether or not it yields to something better, the involuntary forfeit of any set of values always contains an element of tragedy. Beliefs are to society what oxygen is the individual; without them, societies perish. The people of Britain ought to understand this: having invaded, laid waste and undermined whole cultures, secure in the certainty that we were bringing enlightenment and freedom. This is a temptation from which even in the twenty-first century we are by no means immune, as the ruins of Baghdad and Kabul attest. The reason for existence of our town – the leather and shoe industry – was abolished in the 1960s and 70s; and with it, went the compulsions of a working class which was never given recognition while it lived, nor received any acknowledgement when it was extinguished. All this accompanied my mothers sense of dereliction. No wonder she wanted company in her lonely trajectory through all the social dissociations and disruptions that formed the background to her tragic experience. Perhaps this was why she sought all her life to be still – the distances she had covered were immense, the migrations and upheavals vast, even though she never went anywhere.

XI

Sid married again, at least twice. I met his second wife at the golden wedding party of his parents in Olney, our false grandparents, although they, of course, had no inkling that we were unrelated to them. I was then about eighteen; and I rehearsed melodramatic scenes between my self and this woman who, I indignantly imagined, had stolen our father and ruined our family. Should I treat her with scorn, with cold disdain or with sorrowing magnanimity? In the event, she turned out to be a pleasant, homely woman, with a nervous brightness that already suggested premature disillusion with the match she had made; and my blistering remarks went unsaid. When our mother asked what she was like, I said 'It won't last five minutes.' It exceeded five minutes; but not by much.

'He couldn't be tied down', said his mother with a familiar, antique, indulgent connivance in male restlessness. After that, he rented a small terraced house in Olney. This was a squalid place, unadorned by any of the amenities he had enjoyed in his earlier domestic arrangements. I visited him one day. A greasy knuckle of lamb on the table was covered with blow-flies, muddy footprints marked the red flagstones, old letters, cigarette ends and newspaper had been left where they fell. Everything spoke of a weary self-neglect.

His final marriage must have taken place when he was almost sixty. He married a woman who already had several children, and who is said to have observed of her marriage to him that one more would not make much difference. Later, suffering from lung-cancer, he spent nights in his van parked outside the house, because he wanted the fresh air and because he didn't want to disturb his new family with his coughing.

I saw him only once more. He was working for the council as road-sweeper. Thin and old, his hair was crinkled and grey; a cigarette burned on his lips, while he creased his eyes against the sun and smoke. He was pushing a handcart, into which he tipped sweet-papers, fish-and-chip wrappings and dog-shit, which he scooped up with a brush and metal pan. He said to me 'How are you doing at school?' I was twenty seven.

When I heard he was dead it didn't occur to me to go to the funeral. I tried to feel sad, but the best I could do was take refuge in a general feeling of pity at mortality in general. I could find no point of contact with him, neither as the forbidden man who had shared our house, nor as the father I still believed him to be. I could not strike a spark of feeling from the flint of my heart. I thought I must be cold and hard.

Some years later, I spent a summer with my partner at a village near Olney. One evening in the pub, the young woman serving behind the bar said to me 'Are you Jeremy Seabrook?' 'Yes.' She said 'I'm your sister.' I wanted to tell her she was not; but I smiled and said 'I always wanted a sister.' I never saw her again.

XII

My mother was an angry woman, and with good cause. Although to a certain extent, Joe had helped her direct it against disabling social influences, much of it went underground in the traditional guerrilla offensive, which women waged against men by their powerful emotional hold over the children, concern with whom many men still thought was 'women's work'; and they only intervened when there was punishment to be inflicted, which usually meant a good thrashing with the trouser-belt or a stair rod..

My mother's sensibility had been, to a considerable extent, determined by the shoe-making culture of the town. This had a distinctive regional character, rooted in the semi-domestic occupation of shoe- and leather-workers. It may have been the rural origins of their labour, skinning cattle and tanning hides, that preserved something peasant-like in the people. They were stubborn and parsimonious, superstitious; parochial, sceptical and reluctant (or unable) to express feeling. They disagreed with all received wisdom, and were reluctant to believe anything they were told by their betters; actually they recognised no betters. They dissented, even sometimes from quite obvious truths, and they never went with the grain of anything, if they could go against it.

The shoe people were puritanical, unimpressed by money or station, sour, self-righteous, unforgiving but incorruptible. My mother was all of these things. That she remained with her husband through the worst of his sickness until he recovered was characteristic; but that she should continue to punish him till the end equally so.

Their lives seemed to me the most austere sketch of living. I hated the frugality of their unornamented living-rooms, wooden chairs, cold lino and rag rugs, enamel bowls in fireclay sinks, coco matting, women rattling zinc pails and scrubbing immaculate floors with coarse brushes in wide soapy arcs. Their lives were penitential; and even their pleasures – drinking bitter beer, growing sour apples on stony allotments, playing darts and dour philosophy – seemed scarcely less grim than their labour. They saw the world in double negatives. There was nothing to be done without trouble, except letting the fire go out. They wouldn't be surprised to see things get worse before they got better. They didn't believe in being beholden to anybody. There was nothing to be got from pigs but their muck and their company. They bore long grudges; and wouldn't be happy till those who had offended them were singing alleluia to the nettles.

Perhaps because they expected so little, they put up with what ought not to have been tolerated. It was a double misfortune for my mother that she had to live out her solitary drama in circumstances that no longer bore people up by a sharing of hardship or any collective purpose. Even so, I know that, even if her life had been all simplicity and straightforwardness, she would still have been possessed of the same fretful and restless disposition, which is also mine; and her instinct to reject the unexamined wisdom and the miserable orthodoxies of the age has been one of her many gifts to me.

XIII

She had summoned me to her deathbed so often over several decades that it seemed inconceivable that I would not be present when death actually came. I had heard her voice 'Come quick.' 'I need you.' 'I want you.' 'I think this is the end.' 'I feel bad.' Sometimes, between her urgent summons and my arrival, she appeared to have forgotten the urgency of her call, and when I reached her, trembling with anxiety, she would look at me with a troubled frown and say 'You don't generally come on Wednesdays, what's wrong?'

I was in Uttarakhand in North India when she died. As she grew older, I felt that the long grieving for her, which had begun ever before I knew what it was, had exhausted itself. I became more free of her than I had ever been, and was able to leave home for long periods, which had been impossible when I was younger. I also felt the same desire to remain at home, to stay in a safe place. I knew, like her, the attractions of security, the longing for a stillness which became oppressive as soon as it was achieved, the instinct to stay where I was and not risk the perils of the unknown.

The feeling that I had indeed deserted her was strengthened by what I heard from the women of the Himalayan foothills. For they said it is always the men who leave. The men go from the marginal farm, the forest, the hill-side village, into the city. What appears as male enterprise and intrepidity looks different to the women, even though upon their earnings survival depends. Women see their departure as defeat. That is why they go. It is the women who stand and fight the daily war waged against the poor in the home-place, at the most basic level of the struggle for resources.

In a quite different context, my mother was like those women. She had remained. She had endured, and to some extent, salvaged from the devastation of her life, its ruined ecology and wrecked landscape, some dignity, even a silent heroism.

It was a strange experience. I returned to Delhi that night. Towards eleven o'clock, I sat in the dusty hotel room, with its non-functioning TV, bare electric wires plugged into the electric sockets, beneath the cobwebby ceiling in the low-watt gloom. Suddenly the door opened, and an old, old Indian woman walked across the room, as though looking for something. Without uttering a word, she went to the uncurtained window, then turned, and without looking at me, left the room. She had, I assumed, mistaken my room for hers. Yet there was no old woman staying in that corridor. This must have been eight or ten hours after my mother's death. I

The Uses Of Adversity

have never, before or since, had any experience of the paranormal; and I am at a loss to account for this apparition. I can see her still; the dark green saree with the thick cardigan over it against the chill of evening, the silver hair scraped back in a loose bun. I shivered and prepared to take the British Airways flight to London. There was a fault in the aircraft and it stood on the runway for twelve hours; during which time I had time enough to reflect anew on my relationship with my mother.

I thought she would die in the way she had lived, turbulently, angrily, protesting. It was not so. She had a chest infection that failed to respond to antibiotics. The day before she died, she said to the nurses 'Have you sent for my son?' They said yes, but had not thought it necessary. The following afternoon, my cousin was with her, sharing a cup of tea. She sighed and closed her eyes; opened them again to take a last breath. An easy death, everyone said. A lovely way to go. Silent pneumonia. The friend of the old.

When I reached home, I went to see her body. The undertaker made me wait a few minutes, and then he said, rubbing together his dry hands, 'Mother is ready for you now', as though she were his mother too, and she had made the appointment she would keep on her own terms. They had dressed her in a white gown, with silver embroidery and lacy cuffs (had that dainty cerement lain in her wardrobe waiting for this moment?); raiment really, going-to-heaven wear, the robes of her childhood Sunday-school hymns.

I was not overwhelmed by her death as I feared I might be. I thought of the women of the foothills of the Himalayas, labouring in the fields around Haldwani, who had stayed to resist the destruction of their environment. And I understood their kinship with her, my mother, who had remained to resist the inner devastation of her life. I am grateful to her for the insight into the staying-power of women across societies and cultures; women who remain and remember, while men run away and often forget.

Jeremy Seabrook

Jeremy Seabrook
3 Springfield Avenue
London N10 3SU
May 2014
e-mail: yrn63@dial.pipex.com

Printed in Great Britain
by Amazon